A Rainbow Book

Cloud Dancing

Your Introduction to Gliding and Motorless Flight

Robert F. Whelan

Rainbow Books, Inc.

Library of Congress Cataloging-in-Publication Information

Whelan, Robert F., 1949-
    Cloud dancing : your introduction to gliding and motorless flight
  / Robert F. Whelan.
      p. cm.
    ISBN 1-56825-025-8 (acid-free)
    1. Gliding and soaring. 2. Gliders (Aeronautics)--Piloting.
  I. Title.
  TL765.W45 1995
  797.5`5--dc20   95-9807
                                                CIP

Cloud Dancing
Your Introduction to Gliding and Motorless Flight
Copyright 1995 © Robert F. Whelan

Published by Rainbow Books, Inc.
Editorial Offices
P. O. Box 430, Highland City, FL 33846-0430
Phone/Fax (941) 648-4420, E-mail: NAIP@aol.com
Orders: Telephone (800) 356-9315, Fax (800) 242-0036
Cover/interior design by Betsy A. Lampé
Cover photo by Robert F. Whelan

Disclaimer — The material and information presented in this book is intended for the entertainment and edification of the reader. While some of the information may prove helpful to someone seeking to obtain a private pilot's license (glider rating), it is not intended as a substitute for flight instruction.

Manufactured in the United States of America

Dedication

To Sailplane Designers and Flight Instructors everywhere
who make it all possible.

Contents

Introduction

As far back in time as the ancient Greeks, mankind has dreamed of flying like a bird. Mythology tells us Daedalus and Icarus, father and son, built wings patterned after and feathered like birds to escape King Minos' labyrinth. Thousands more years were to pass before mankind's dreams were realized, and in that time the dream lost none of its power, none of its allure. Today, perhaps the closest man has come to realizing this dream is with modern-day gliders — sleek airplanes without engines — airplanes capable, in the right hands and given the right conditions, of remaining aloft literally as long as the wind blows, of soaring over a thousand miles without landing, of climbing above 50,000 feet, of crossing the Mediterranean Sea. All this from a tow behind a light powerplane of only 2,000 feet above the ground.

This book is one very lucky man's tribute to the sport of soaring, a sport he has been privileged to participate in almost since the day he began his working life. In more than 20 years since that time, flying primarily on weekends, he progressed from knowing almost nothing about soaring to being able to remain aloft as long as he chooses — some of the time! — after each release from the towplane. Had he imagined current skills in mind's eye 20 years ago, he might have wondered if, in the future, the sport might get too easy, if some of the magic might be lost. The hypothetical question has a very real answer: So long as I am blessed with reasonably good health, I expect to continue soaring in the 3-dimensional ocean of air above my head. For today, if anything, my samplings of mankind's dream have only whetted my appetite for more.

Gaining today's experience wasn't always easy, it wasn't always satisfying, and very occasionally it wasn't even fun. But only once did I consider not continuing with the sport because, for me, the simple satisfaction of realizing a child's dream of piloting any aircraft through the skies has evolved into something more. Ever since my first sailplane ride in 1972, the people I've met and the situations I've seen — literally, my views of the world — have been colored by my participation in the physically and spiritually uplifting sport of soaring.

Should the reader ever have wondered at the freedom birds experience, of the sensations of flight in a medium they call home as much as the earth is to us, and if they've wondered: *Could I ever experience some of these things?*, this book is an attempt to provide some answers. And if it also helps fire your dreams, and encourage in some small way translation of those dreams to reality, it will have served its purpose. Whatever the case, may you gain by reading it some of the pleasure and understanding the sport is capable of bestowing.

Chapter One

Why?

Dreams, how powerful they can be! From nowhere originates human thoughts, motivations, concepts, often beyond
rational comprehension. Why are these so powerful? Why
their tenacious grip on our spirits? What is it about flight
that has historically attracted man with a power, all too
often in the beginning, exceeding the very force of life itself? The answers to such questions lie deep within our very
beings, as varied as each of us are unique. But there's no
denying humankind's ages-old desire to soar aloft like a bird.

From the centuries-old myth of Icarus to the many
sketches of Leonardo da Vinci 500 years ago, from the
Montgolfier brothers' first man-carrying balloons in revo-
lutionary times right up until the twentieth century, men
dreamed, sketched and strove to fly. Unrelenting failure,
even death, did nothing to lessen the power of the dream.
When man could not join the birds directly, he attempted
to join them indirectly, seeking the advantages inherent in
height. Historically, these advantages usually had more to
with death, destruction and war than esthetics, and not
until this century was mankind able to begin seriously emu-
lating birds for simple enjoyment's sake. A few short years

after its invention, the hot-air balloon was usurped by armies to spy on opposing armies. Walled cities have always employed high towers for observation and defense. Even the powered airplane ultimately underwent great advances under the impetus of wars, while gliders were used by both sides to transport troops and supplies into combat during World War II.

But despite winged death, destruction from on high, and the perversion of every kind of flying machine ever made for mean-spirited purposes, for the common man the dream of flight remains deep-rooted. It may be truthfully said flight has a certain mystique to it, even in today's frenetically changing, techno-whiz world. Airplane crashes, large and small, always make the news. The nonstop, unrefueled 'round-the-world flight of the *Voyager,* by Dick Rutan and Jeana Yeager, captured the industrialized world's attention as had few things since space flight. Hollywood continues a long history of perpetuating the myth of superman as pilot with movies like *Top Gun.* Any pilot can instantly change the topic at dull social gatherings by casually mentioning he or she flies. Whether for a living or for fun doesn't matter.

The Wright brothers had a dream of simple, powered flight. They sincerely believed their invention might forever mean the end of wars; they foresaw a time when air travel would shrink the world so much that reasonable men would understand all men were brothers, and they would modify their behavior such that all might live in peace. Only after four years of pursuing their dream under hard, lonely conditions, did they make the first, short flight today's world remembers most.

Charles Lindbergh had a dream to connect Europe and the U.S., to shrink the Atlantic, to bind foreign peoples more closely. The achievement of his dream became possible only after months of fund-raising, helping design *The Spirit of St. Louis* and arduous study of navigation.

Successful pursuit of Dick Rutan's and Jeana Yeager's dream took them over six years. No less pioneers than

Wilbur, Orville and Lindbergh, like them, their plane was designed by an individual — not a large company. Similarly, the *Voyager* came into being only through the efforts of a very few individuals who hand-built it on a shoestring budget. And ultimately, like those with dreams before them, they risked their lives pursuing *their* dream.

Dreams, whether grand or humble, deserve to be pursued. They inspire us beyond the ordinary tasks of daily living. They refresh our minds. They make life more alive.

So strongly does the dream of flight grip many, even today, that in countless garages throughout the U.S., otherwise normal people pursue their dreams of flight by hand-crafting their own flying machines. Thousands successfully take to the air each year.

We are fortunate to live in a time and place where, if our dreams of flight are to join the birds wheeling gracefully, effortlessly, above our heads, we may — with moderate tenacity and normal skills — realize them. Few among us have not gazed aloft on a lazy summer day, or a day at the beach, and envied the birds with their freedom of travel, their easy mastery of three-dimensional space, their ability to view the world from on high. And who among us cannot recall childhood's nocturnal dreams of flight? Happily today, the choices for such dreamers abound in the United States. Within easy driving distance of major population centers throughout the lower 48 states and Hawaii, one can find locations to take hot-air balloon rides, introductory flights in power planes, dual rides in hang gliders and paragliders, and soaring rides. A quick trip into the *Yellow Pages* can be followed by one to a flight center where the itch to fly can be scratched.

At commercial soaring centers, gift rides — birthday, anniversary, Christmas — are commonly available. Some sites even have sailplanes which can take two passengers aloft simultaneously in the cozy rear seat of the glider, although most sailplanes can carry but one. For those lucky enough to have a contact, members of soaring clubs often provide rides to friends and potential club members in club two seaters.

Of all the avenues into the sky available today, the sport of soaring arguably comes the closest to allowing humans to experience what it must be like to be a bird. Once free from the light plane or winch required to tow the glider aloft, sailplanes — also called gliders, the terms being used interchangeably — slip almost noiselessly through the sky, in harmony with nature and the birds. There isn't a sailplane pilot in the land who can't recall with reverent delight one or more encounters with soaring hawks and eagles. So at one with nature are these graceful creations of man, that researchers use sailplanes to study soaring birds "on their own turf." Though the gliders of today fly much faster than soaring birds fly, making it difficult to remain in the same air as a hawk or eagle when gliding in a straight line, when both must circle in lift to ascend, climb rates are similar, and the thrill of thermalling with eagles will not soon be forgotten.

The sky is such a big place that, while it's unlikely you'll join with an eagle on your first flight, anything is possible, and if the author's years of quite unscientific observations and surveys of people returning from their first rides are any measure, it will make no difference! Rare, indeed, is the person whose expectations aren't met by their first ride in a sailplane.

Come along on an introductory ride into the realm of birds and bird men.

Chapter Two

What Should I Expect?

If you've ever thought of going for a sailplane ride or of taking soaring lessons, take heart. To take a ride, nothing more is needed than a phone to make the appointment, the disposable cash to purchase the flight, and the ability to reach a gliderport on a flyable day. Bear in mind the sport is eternally slave to the vagaries of weather. Lessons are within your grasp if you are of average coordination, have a healthy respect for the fragility of your body, are persistent and are motivated.

If you do decide to take the adventure of an introductory ride, there are a few simple things you can do to enhance the experience. Most importantly, dress for sun; a soft hat with a small sun brim and no button on top is best. Also, take a camera or VCR, for bringing friends to the airport to share the excitement of your first ride is highly recommended! Plan on making it at least a half-day expedition; you won't want to feel rushed. For unlike those modern people-funnels familiar to any commercial air traveler — so dreadfully efficient it's easy to never see what the plane you're flying on actually looks like — sport airports are different. Here, you won't find bored security guards, armed police, barbed-wire-topped chain-link fences, or trained dogs. You're much more likely to encounter helpful, friendly people who encourage you, your family and friends to pull up a picnic table, watch and chat. And the only dog you'll see may be some humble airport dog, usually a nondescript mongrel who's decided it, too, likes airplanes, pilots and their friends.

The cost of a ride might range from approximately $50 to $150 depending on location, length, number of people riding in the sailplane and what you want to do. Dual flights and aerobatic flights (which require a higher tow) cost more than a basic introductory soaring flight, on which you'll typically tow to 3,000 feet above the earth. Total flight time of a typical introductory flight will be approximately 30 minutes, most of that coming after release from tow. Actual altitude and duration will depend upon weather conditions at the time and — sometimes — your stomach.

You Made It!

What you'll find upon arrival at a typical gliderport is a simple parking lot, rarely paved, a small operations building (or trailer or two), a row of surprisingly small, notably engineless gliders and some equally small single-engined lightplanes growling about. Pretty humble stuff. Any fence will obviously be designed less to prevent terrorist trespass than to prevent the confused wandering of a curious onlooker's car onto an active runway. Gliderports are almost always based on airports at which any kid on a bicycle would be welcomed. Right about then your serious second thoughts may begin!

Ignore them long enough to find the simple, inevitable observation deck, buttonhole someone who works for the glider operation and begin asking questions. They'll be happy to answer them, or, if occupied with some preexisting task, point you toward someone who can help. If your arrival coincides with a time when the deck is occupied only by friends of people aloft for rides, chat with these folks. If the deck's empty, enjoy the proceedings and watch everyone perform their flying jobs; someone will be by soon enough.

The most pressing questions of people upon arrival at a gliderport, expecting to put their exquisitely valuable bodies into the contraption and hands of another, concern safety. Right up front, the author must apologize for a personal bias too strong not to color the following information. The bias is that he believes life itself is a risk. The only guarantee any of us have about our lives is that they will eventually end. In the author's view, managing life-threatening risks is one key to raising the odds that the end of a person's life will coincide with natural causes . . . presumably everyone's goal!

Riding in a car without a seat belt or riding a motorcycle without a helmet are unquestionably riskier than using those protections, regardless of state laws. So is riding in a motorboat without flotation devices for the boat and occupants. Knitting, as a hobby, is safer than ski-jumping or rock climbing or bicycle riding or fishing or roller-blading. And, of course, probably the most statistically dangerous activity any of us routinely pursue is automobile travel.

But only when we are about to undertake a new experience do we ever typically consider the risks, even if only in passing. For most activities, risk management is left up to the individual. Flying is different. For better or worse, every heavier-than-air craft which flies in U.S. skies comes (except for some of the lighter and slower-flying ultralight craft) under federal government attempts to manage many of the risks inherent to flight. The Federal Aviation Agency (the *Feds*, the *FAA*) has legal authority over all soaring flight in the U.S. Through its Federal Aviation Regulations (the *FARs*), the Feds set the rules for all gliders and all glider pilots, just as they do for all commercial aviation.

What this means to the trusting non-pilot wishing to take a glider ride is that their expectations of safety when boarding a glider ought be no different than those they have when boarding a commercial jet. You should expect to return safely. Each glider and each pilot will meet certain standards and guidelines. There's no guarantee meeting these guidelines will result in a perfectly safe flight, of course, but the statistics show commercial glider operations are exceedingly safe. The simple fact of the matter is the most dangerous aspect of any activity, which takes you higher than you're willing to fall or sends you faster than you're willing to hit a brick wall, is the person in charge of the activity. Experience without sound judgment is a recipe for disaster; inexperience and good judgment, on the other hand, is a formula for a lifetime of enjoyment.

When it comes to flying, few pilots have such poor judgment that they intentionally put *passengers* at risk. As for them putting passengers *unintentionally* at risk, the FARs do an effective job of minimizing this. Before a person can obtain a license allowing him to carry paying glider passengers, he must have at least 100 hours as pilot in command of a glider, be able to fly and land the glider with greater precision than was required for him to obtain his private glider license, and pass a second set of written and flying tests. All flying exams are taken under the auspices of a pilot who has qualified to even more stringent rules.

You might be surprised to learn that gliders are actually stronger than the typical light plane, which in turn can withstand accelerations greater than can commercial passenger jets. All gliders can safely perform limited aerobatics (e.g. loops, rolls), while some are specifically strengthened for more strenuous aerobatics. No aerobatics are legal unless both pilot and passenger wear parachutes. Also (not that your pilot would ever do this), it might be reassuring to know that the glider you ride in is unlikely to fly faster than a certain speed — called *maneuvering speed* by engineering types. Below maneuvering speed, the pilot can move the controls as violently and vigorously as humanly possible, to the full limit of their travel, and the plane will suffer no ill effects. Above maneuvering speed, it's theoretically possible to pull the wings off any plane, including commercial jets. (You can recognize maneuvering speed by the upper end of the green arc on the airspeed indicator of the glider you ride in; typically it will be around 90 m.p.h.)

The gliders (and the towplanes) are also inspected — and any substandard conditions corrected before being returned to service — by a licensed airplane mechanic at least once each year.

Still a little uncertain about things? Ask your pilot how much glider time he has. Anything over about 400 hours is quite a lot of experience in sailplanes; many commercial glider pilots have thousands of hours in gliders and, sometimes, many additional hours in powerplanes. In any case, don't worry too much about being nervous. Such nervousness shows you have a normal, healthy fear of the unknown!

Your Magic Carpet

The glider you'll ride in is likely to be one of four types, and, unless you're riding double, you'll be in the front seat, of course.

Probably most common nowadays is a German-built, fiberglass two-seater called a Grob (pronounced *Grobe*). Representative of current sailplane technology, Grobs are sleek (sexy?), white gliders with decadent, semi-reclined, upholstered tandem seats.

Still common are all-metal, American-designed and built Schweizer 2-32's. The highest performance two seater in the world when it was designed in the 1960s, like all Schweizer gliders, the 2-32 is also a stout, rugged design. More graceful in appearance than many Schweizers, some people think its huge canopy — which provides unparalleled visibility — a bit bulbous. The 2-32 is the only sport glider in the world which can carry three aloft, but only if the two passengers' combined weight is less than 300 pounds, and it's best if the two passengers are good friends, for the rear seat with two aboard is quite cozy. Couples typically enjoy riding together in the 2-32.

Less common is another two-person, metal design called the *Blanik*. Interestingly, *Blaniks* are a Czechoslovakian design of the same era as the 2-32. They are instantly recognizable by their swept-forward wings and bullet-shaped wingtip 'tanks,' which are actually there just for looks. *Blaniks* resulted from the Czechs' desire at the time to develop an aerospace industry. A communist nation in those cold war times, for reasons of simplicity their leaders decided to make the new industry's first design a glider. Consequently, *Blaniks* have flaps, semi-retractable landing gear and spoilers, all designed to get Czech pilots used to all the handles they would encounter in subsequent jet training. Too good a glider to be used exclusively for military training, several hundred *Blaniks* were imported into the U.S. as sport gliders, and for years the plane held a number of two-seat, world soaring records.

Probably the least commonly used glider to give introductory rides is another Schweizer design, the 2-33. This is the glider which trained a generation of U.S. glider pilots before twin Grobs began to displace them. Although a superb thermal soaring machine, because of its decidedly utilitarian if not pedestrian appearance, many people are reluctant to take their initial rides in 2-33s. This is something of a shame since, if you desire, your pilot will happily let you handle the flight controls on your ride, and, thanks to its being a training ship, in the 2-33 you're most likely to be able to actually do well enough to gain altitude if you locate a thermal. The higher-performance gliders require more skill to thermal efficiently than a beginner typically brings to the cockpit.

Each of these four gliders weighs between 600 and 850 pounds, ready for pilot and passenger. Each also has a full set of controls in front and back cockpits; Grobs and *Blaniks* also have dual sets of instrumentation, while the Schweizers' instruments are arranged so any pilot flying from the rear seat can easily view airspeed, altimeter and variometer from behind the passenger.

Regardless of which type of glider you take your first ride in, it will prove a memorable experience!

Here We Go!

Once you've made connections with your pilot, he or she may ask for your help pulling the glider onto the runway. Again, don't be afraid to ask for directions; typically your help will be needed to level a wingtip while the pilot pushes or pulls the plane from its tiedown to the runway. Once the glider is in the takeoff position comes the big moment — getting into it! Your pilot will show you how to do this without harming the sailplane. When you take this step, you've crossed a major philosophic hurdle. It's one thing to decide, in the comfort of your own home, that you want to take a glider ride. It's quite another to actually strap one on. And, unless you're riding alone in a 2-32 (in which case you'll be surprised by how roomy it is), that's what it'll seem like you're doing since, in the interest of performance, glider cockpits are made no larger than necessary. You'll find a single-width seat with hip and shoulder belts; in aerobatic twin Grobs there will be a fifth crotch strap. Each strap snaps into a central, quick-release type buckle, with which your pilot will help you as you put the plane on. Ready for flight, your hips and torso will be comfortably restrained against the seat, but your head, arms and legs will be free for normal movement.

If the day is hot, your pilot will allow you to keep your canopy open until immediately before takeoff, then describe how to close and lock it. From his seat in the back, he can visually verify you've done it properly. If you and a friend are riding together in the rear seat of a 2-32, your pilot will close the vast single-piece canopy then turn his head to verify the rear locking pin is properly engaged.

Before entering the cockpit, your pilot will probably connect a metal ring on the end of the towrope to a release on the outside of the glider, near its nose; he may ask for your help operating the *interior tow release knob* when doing this. Sometimes a third person will be available to connect the towrope, in which case your pilot will strap in and operate the tow release knob directly while the helper handles the rope. As with the glider, the strength of the rope and the *weak link* at the glider end are subject to federal regulations. Typically, most operations use an overly strong rope to avoid having to change them frequently due to abrasion from dragging on the ground. They then put a weak link between the rope and the glider. The purpose of the weak link is to ensure it will break *before* damage to towplane or glider occurs in the event the glider somehow gets out of position on tow and gives a healthy yank to the rope. Student pilots yank on ropes a lot! On your flight, the rope will no doubt appear to be rigid, as experienced pilots have no trouble flying proper formation behind the tug.

Once the rope is connected, both of you are strapped in, and both canopies are closed and locked, the glider is ready for takeoff. First though, the towplane pilot must remove all slack from the rope, which is done by slowly taxiing forward. You may feel some slight forward movement of the glider when the slack comes out. Immediately after the rope is taut, your pilot will alternately press each rudder pedal beneath your feet to the floor, waggling the glider's rudder from side to side. The tug pilot, seeing this waggle in a rearview mirror, knows that both of you are ready for takeoff and applies full power to the towplane.

With a startling surge, the two of you will accelerate down the runway, the tug — for some — astonishingly close at the end of the 180-200 foot rope. Faster than your unattuned senses can easily appreciate, the rising whirr of the wheel close beneath your seat will begin to diminish the instant you lift off the runway. You'll do this while the tug is still rolling along the ground, accelerating to its slightly higher flying speed. After your glider lifts off, the pilot will hold it close above the ground directly behind the towplane, maintaining this position relative to the tug throughout the rest of the tow.

You're actually flying *formation* with the towplane. Formation flying is something few pilots, outside of those in the military, and airshow teams, ever get to do. It's a normal part of glider flying, and once they get the hang of it, glider pilots usually enjoy the challenge and visual aspects of towing. It's one of the times when you can really *see* that airplanes fly through an ever-shifting ocean of air. Notice how glider and tug are always in slight relative motion to each other; this is due to the towplane being two or three seconds ahead of the air of the glider. If the tug rises, moments later, so will your glider.

Right now, during the takeoff roll, and again during the final landing approach, is when real skill is needed to safely fly the glider. Aloft, free of the towplane, far from anything you can hit, precision affects only your ability to soar, not your safety.

Joining the Birds

As the earth begins to sink away from you and you encounter atmospheric motion, notice how the glider feels more like a cork bobbing on water than a car jolting across speed bumps. This oddly squishy motion results from the long wings and the relatively low flying speed of the glider. If you're riding in a Grob, you can even look along the wings and see a graceful bow in them; they will flex gently in the slightest turbulence, actually smoothing the ride some more, much as if you were suspended on a rubber band. This is a normal characteristic of fiberglass sailplanes. Metal-winged gliders are similar, except for the absence of apparent wing-bowing. You'll be able to hear their wings flexing, though, as the aluminum skins *oilcan* in all but the lightest turbulence. *Bwornka, bwornka, bwornk.* It's normal, and most glider pilots soon think of it as kind of soothing!

Regardless of your previous flight experiences, whether in commercial jet or light power plane, you'll be able to more directly *feel* what the air is doing in a glider than in any other sort of airplane. Even though, when compared to birds, humans are woefully adapted to use these sensations of movement to help them soar, experienced glider pilots often develop a sixth sense which helps them detect lift or sink before it shows on the *variometer*, normally the primary soaring instrument. But even the best soaring pilots rely primarily on their instruments to help them locate and stay in lift.

Directly ahead of you, taped to the outside of the canopy, will be the least expensive, most sensitive and one of the most important soaring instruments available. It's a short piece of yarn or string, called a *yaw string*. Because air is so thin, and the plane's controls are so powerful, it's an easy thing to do to make the plane fly through the air skidding sideways. By always keeping the yaw string pointed back toward the tail, glider pilots avoid the extra drag of such uncoordinated flight. Any plane without a propeller up front can benefit from a yaw string, and you might be surprised to know that both the U-2 spy plane and the supersonic F-14 Tomcat use yaw strings. U-2 pilots use them for the same reason glider pilots use them, for in essence the U-2 is an exotic, powered glider. F-14 pilots use them to tweak their throttles to develop equal amounts of thrust at 100% power settings. Since their engines are nine feet apart, and, because no two engines ever develop exactly the same amount of power, the planes would permanently fly sideways a bit without their Mach II yarn to assist the pilot!

While you're still attached to the towplane, notice how your horizon expands wonderfully as the earth sinks away! Many find it simultaneously the most normal thing in the world, yet a completely new and marvelous experience. Oddly, despite the panoramic view incomparably better than the view through any window of a commercial jet, despite being able to look almost straight down past either shoulder to the ground below, even acrophobes almost never experience fear of heights riding in sailplanes. Rare indeed is the person who doesn't thoroughly enjoy their first experience riding in a sailplane on tow.

Still, there are those whose fears or inner ears send alarm signals to their stomachs at some point in the flight, so perhaps a little foreknowledge can lessen any tendency you might have toward motion sickness. Although no pilot ever intentionally tries to make a passenger sick to his stomach, it sometimes happens. In fact, some experienced *pilots* fight a tendency toward airsickness their entire lives! The author used to think adult motion sickness was entirely fear-induced until he encountered pilots absolutely hooked on flying who consistently got sick after an hour or two of flight. But rarely does queasiness come on so rapidly that you can't alert your pilot to return to earth before it becomes critical. Regardless, *sick sacks* are always carried, and, happily, most people quite rapidly feel much improved should they succumb.

There are a few tricks you can use to minimize the newness of all the visual impressions flooding in upon you, inducing motion sickness. One is to simply hold your head level; don't lean into turns and don't twist your head into awkward positions attempting to see something. Second, direct your gaze toward the horizon. Looking at distant objects, rather than nearby things which appear to be moving more rapidly relative to you, settles the world down considerably. Third, when you do move your head, do it in a smooth, steady motion to give time for the fluid in your ears' circular canals to adapt somewhat.

On almost everyone's first ride in a glider, they draw upon their bicycle experience and lean the direction the plane is turning. There's no need to do this in airplanes. In fact, no matter how steep the turn (or *bank*, as it's called in aviation), if it's a coordinated one (and if you want to go soaring, all turns in gliders should be!), with closed eyes, you wouldn't be able to tell you were in a turn at all until it became quite steep and you began to weigh more as the force of the turn pressed you more heavily into the seat. If you've ever whirled a bucket of water about your head as a kid, you no doubt noticed it got heavier and heavier the faster it swung. The same sort of force acting to keep the water in the bucket acts on people in turning airplanes; that's why passenger jets aren't steeply banked . . . to do everything possible to insulate the passengers from the sen-

sation of flight!

A marble on a level, flat plate would remain in the center of the plate during coordinated turns. A full glass of tea resting on the instrument panel would not spill. Further, leaning into turns seriously confuses your circular canals, and can induce *vertigo* (the sensation of dizziness) and motion sickness in an otherwise unaffected passenger.

Your tow will probably last between five and ten minutes. In a surprisingly short time, you'll have reached your *release altitude*. Undoubtedly your pilot will alert you to the impending transition to pure gliding flight and may even ask you to operate the tow release knob. Regardless of who operates the release knob, be prepared for a loud *CRACK!* when the release is pulled. It will sound like something has broken, and the towplane will probably lurch up on one wing and fall for the ground as if you just shot it down. Don't worry! Everything is normal. The release makes the loud noise, and towpilots get to have their fun after you release; they love to perform steep slips back to the landing pattern. To the untrained eye, a steep slip looks like an impending crash. If you can keep your eye on the towplane, you'll see he slips back toward the airport on his way to a normal landing and the next tow.

As for you and your sailplane, why, it's time to go soaring!

Chapter Three

Cloud Dancing

The sky is a remarkably alive place, though few of us ever give much thought to just how vibrant it is. For most, grumbling about rain spoiling a picnic or hoping for snow to ski is about as far as our thoughts wander. For the soaring pilot, though, the sky becomes a place to park a portion of his waking brain because knowledge and awareness of the sky are his primary assets in the ceaseless hunt to remain aloft after release — to soar. From March through October, anywhere throughout the U.S. on any given day, it will likely be possible to soar some time during that day. In mountainous terrain, it's possible to soar year 'round. So odds are, if the weather is good enough for you to take an introductory tow, your chances of finding *lift* are pretty good.

If your flight takes place in the more humid air, east of a line extending north through central Texas, on a decent soaring day you'll have a good chance of dancing with the clouds. In the drier air, farther west, cloud dancing is less likely but, in return, lift there tends to be stronger and go higher. Still, nothing is free — lift is also farther apart out west!

No matter where one takes a soaring ride, however, once free from the towplane, and in order to soar, the sailplane pilot must think and fly like any soaring bird. For, like soaring birds, sailplanes constantly convert height into forward speed in order to generate the flow around the wings necessary to sustain their weight. Soaring birds and sailplanes are always gliding downhill, down an invisible slope. When birds attempting to soar fail to locate air rising more rapidly than they are sinking, they can choose to flap. Gliders cannot, so they must either find and remain within an area of rising air or glide to the inevitable landing.

With the twin advantages of experience and hindsight, some glider pilots eventually conclude finding and using this rising air — *lift* — is unremarkably simple because there's so much of it! Yet, while the principles behind soaring flight have become clear if not simple in ninety plus years of human experience, gaining the individual piloting skill to effectively utilize both principles and lift is not. To the untrained eye, the difference between a sailplane pilot who is a competent and safe pilot and one who is these things, as well as a capable *soaring* pilot, is indistinguishable. But when it comes to results, there's no contest — soaring is an activity in which there's no substitute for experience!

What this means to you, if you want to maximize your chances of actually soaring on your introductory flight, is it'll be best to let your pilot handle the controls. If you're more interested in learning how the plane actually flies, you can handle the controls in all safety, but *you* probably won't be able to soar. On a really good day, the two of you can do both: your pilot soaring until it's time to land, and you flying until you've glided the plane down to the landing pattern, at which point your pilot will retake the controls.

This Thing Called a Thermal

If you choose to attempt to soar, be prepared for a lot of circling unless you're flying alongside a ridge. In a subsequent chapter, the nature of convective lift will be explored in more detail. For now, just note that, when air is heated, it tends to rise in columns called *thermals*, much as steam from a teakettle's spout does. Sometimes you can see thermals from swirling leaves or dust trapped within them. Most people would just as soon *not* see nature's strongest thermals, tornadoes, but the inverted funnel shape of tornado clouds is typical of the shape of most thermals. Narrow near the ground and wider aloft.

The size of typical thermals is small enough to require gliders to continuously circle in order to remain within their rising confines. It's this turning, which appears leisurely if not downright lazy viewed from the ground, which creates the common image in people's minds of gliders wafting aimlessly through the sky. Nothing could be farther from the truth.

In addition to being relatively narrow, many thermals tend to have a strong central core, while others feel exactly like the smoke from an explosion or a large fire looks — roiled and billowing with multiple cores. Broad, gentle, coreless thermals are quite uncommon. Consequently, the most efficient use of thermal lift requires steep banks, often with constantly varying bank angles, in surprisingly turbulent air. But the return is magnificent! A well-flown, strong, eastern thermal can easily lift straight up half a ton of glider and passengers at vertical speeds exceeding ten m.p.h.! Out west, 20 m.p.h. thermals are not uncommon. And in parts of the country where they burn stubble fields, heat from these fires can throw gliders skyward at speeds exceeding 35 m.p.h.! Stubble field fires are so violent that most glider pilots refuse to enter them unless everything in the cockpit is securely fastened down (including the pilot!), all air vents are closed and they are wearing their oxygen masks. It isn't unusual to see burning stubble zooming past the glider thousands of feet above the ground.

Of course, the glider is actually flying around 45-50 m.p.h. in thermalling climbs, and the instrument which shows how fast you're rising or sinking (the variometer) is calibrated in hundreds of feet per minute rather than miles per hour, but there's no mistaking when you fly into a strong thermal! It's a real kick . . . in one's seat!

Thermals aren't usually encountered straight on. Rather, so intimately at home in the sky are sailplanes, that one long wing or the other will be thrust aloft when it first pokes into rising air. The glider will actually attempt to turn *away* from thermals if left to its own devices. All sailplane pilots quickly develop a conditioned reflex which immediately forces the rising wing back down as they enter a bank toward any suspected thermal. Often around the perimeter of the rising air column will be a band of turbulent mixing air, the *transition zone* between the thermal and the larger surrounding area of less active air. So, on your flight, the first sign you're nearing a thermal is likely to be a sudden shaking, much as if the glider is suddenly flying over cobblestones. To a glider pilot, the more the air moves, the better his chances of encountering organized lift. As a result, the bumps aren't viewed with alarm but with anticipation. Expect your pilot's voice to rise half an octave in excited anticipation when he thinks you're nearing lift, since, no matter how experienced a pilot is, the thrill of climbing "for free" never lessens!

Watch the variometer when you roll into a thermalling turn. If the pilot has guessed correctly, before the first half of the turn is complete, the glider will have begun to rise relative to the ground and the vario needle will point to how fast. Not long after, the *altimeter* will show you're gaining altitude. *You're soaring!* Now look directly above the sailplane for a cloud; often the tops of thermals are marked by puffy *cumulus* clouds. It takes time for air rising from the ground to reach the cooler air aloft, which condenses out the humidity in the air to form the cloud. If you don't see one right away, and other parts of the sky are dotted with cumulus clouds, check again every few minutes.

Clouds are a soaring pilot's sky map; they make his job of interpreting where areas of lift and sink might be found much simpler than it would be in a totally blue sky. But there can be lift in the complete absence of clouds, too, particularly on low-humidity days. On such days, all the sailplane pilot can do is fly straight ahead until he bumps into a thermal, much as a blindfolded person might do walking through a woods. Soaring on these *blue days* can be psychologically easier for a pilot, since he has less decisions to make in the search for thermals. But *centering* them is largely a matter of guesswork. Newer soaring pilots often experience frustration trying to center thermals on blue days, since there are no cloud clues to aid the decision of which way to bank.

Clouds or no clouds, once a thermal is located after release from tow, all sailplane pilots work diligently to position the glider in the strongest area of lift. This centering of the lift is done by altering the bank angle, and thus the glider's track, until a constant bank angle results in a more or less constant rate of climb all the way around the circle. Only truly well-behaved thermals permit hands-off thermalling flight; much more commonly it's necessary to adjust the bank angle several times around the turn in order to maximize the time the glider spends in the strongest areas of lift. The ability to make these continuous adjustments is another skill separating tigers from tyros.

Some thermals are so narrow and ill-defined that the glider will be in lift a portion of the turn and then sink during the remainder. Whether or not the pilot elects to fight with these sort of thermals depends both on how badly he needs the altitude and his perception of the likelihood of the thermal improving or worsening. Generally, the closer to the ground, the worse the sort of lift the pilot will accept. Higher up, the glider pilot can afford to pick and choose only the strongest thermals, gliding right on through the weaker ones.

With luck, your thermal will be relatively broad and smooth, permitting an easy bank angle and a steady climb. As you rise, you'll notice air coming through the glider's vents becoming pleasantly cool, and, if a cloud forms atop your thermal, soon you'll be in its soothing shade. One of the attractions of the sport for some is the fact that the hottest hours of the hottest days of summer are spent in nature's air-conditioned splendor! As you near the cloud's base, look at the sky around you and notice how the bottoms of other clouds are more or less at the same elevation. Remember how it looks, for these are classic soaring conditions!

More distant clouds will appear quite flat-bottomed, with sharply defined edges. Nearby clouds will have a more ragged appearance to their bottoms, while your cloud may appear downright nondescript, with a dirty, gray bottom, an ill-defined base and, sometimes, an inverted bowl-shaped bottom surface. Judging vertical distances from clouds is quite difficult; typically, they initially appear much closer than they actually are. Your pilot will attempt to maintain at least 500 feet of *clearance* between the glider and the bottom of the cloud, per regulations, but what he or she will really be doing is maintaining clear *visual contact* with the ground and the sky surrounding the cloud. The purpose of the regulation is to prevent two things: collision with other aircraft and loss of control due to loss of visual contact with the ground. Even birds can't remain under control in dense clouds; they need to see just like us.

Therefore, if you're climbing with a hawk, odds are he'll leave the thermal before entering the cloud.

And, well before the cloud can envelop the glider, your pilot will probably gleefully roll out on a course traversing the entire bottom of the cloud — which will seem much larger than you first guessed, now that you're near it — fly through the wide top of the thermal (gaining speed all the way), until, as you burst back into brilliant, glorious sunlight, he can zoom up along the side of the cloud in a climbing turn. Gazing through the top of the canopy at the impossibly white, billowy, soft sides of nearby cumulus clouds is an experience to be treasured! If you're really fortunate, lift may extend beyond your cloud's perimeter, permitting you to soar up along the cloud's face — sometimes even above it.

At these times, look for a "*sun dog*": a circular rainbow enclosing a glowing, lemon-yellow disk of light, at the very center of which will be a perfectly-formed shadow of your sailplane! This is one of the many visual wonders nature serves up so unexpectedly to the soaring pilot. It will race you to the cloud's edge, leaping joyously from nearby billow to distant hollow, perhaps vanishing for the briefest instant of light and shadow, dimming with distance, brightening with nearness, as infinitely tempting as the pot o' gold at the end of an earthly rainbow.

Whether cloud dancing with a friendly fair-weather cumulus cloud, or the vast, humbling, ethereal beauty of a high-altitude *lenticular* cloud, the experience burns itself vividly into memory — not one to soon be forgotten. No artist's palette can begin to compare with the brilliance, diversity and *intensity* nature routinely crafts into clouds' colors. Regardless of how often pilots can enjoy nature's cloud spectaculars from a cockpit, and from gliders it has a certain privilege value to it, only the most deadened sense of wonder isn't affected.

Off We Go . . .

The time must come to regretfully leave your initial thermal. What next? If the day is a good one, you might have sufficient altitude to fly cross-country in search of a second on-course thermal. You won't actually go beyond gliding distance of the airport on an introductory ride but, often, you easily could. Instead, your pilot will probably offer now *to let you fly the glider* if you wish. Be brave! Do it! You won't be allowed to get yourself into any danger, and you'll begin to learn the secret to most soaring: Letting the glider do the work.

The sailplane will happily fly itself at its trimmed speed, requiring from you only a nudge in this direction or that when you wish to add some intelligence to its blind wanderings. One of the secrets to training flight is to lighten up on the controls: the smoother the air, the smoother the hand on the stick. It's for this reason that training is usually done in the calmer air of morning, thus allowing the student to more easily distinguish between beginning hamfistedness and unwanted motions induced by the atmosphere, for which he must correct.

You, of course, will want to experiment with turns in either direction and possibly do some "zoomies" in your aerial roller coaster. You'll find operation of the stick quite natural: Move it forward and the glider goes faster, pull it back toward you, and it climbs briefly while slowing down. Move it to the right and the plane banks right, beginning to turn that direction. Same thing in the other direction. In essence, the stick is a combination throttle and steering wheel. You can fly the glider with one hand.

So, what about your feet? What are they used for in a sailplane? It is unlike a sled, on which your feet steer by pressing on a steering bar. Even though the pedals beneath your feet *are* connected to a rudder at the rear of the plane, this rudder does not make the plane turn. Boat drivers have particular problems understanding the difference between a boat's rudder — which *does* make the boat turn — and an airplane's rudder, which simply *coordinates* the turn. All your feet do in a sailplane is press on whichever rudder pedal they must in order to keep the yaw string pointed as straight back toward the tail as possible.

Try a turn without using the rudder pedals while watching the yaw string. Say you wish to turn right. Move the stick to the right and the wings bank to the right, in response, and begin pulling the plane around in a turn to the right. But what's this? The nose first slewed to the left, making the yaw string point to your left shoulder, not the tail! Do it again if you're not certain what you saw.

Without coordinating rudder, the nose will initially yaw left before it eventually ends up pointing the yaw string back at the tail again. Roll into another right turn, this time pressing on the right rudder pedal the same time you move the stick. If your foot pressure is just right, the yaw string will remain pointed back at the tail as you roll into this turn. You've just made a *coordinated turn*, and the rudder is what allowed you to do it.

Even if you've flown a power plane before, odds are you won't use enough rudder when first attempting to fly a glider. The need for lots of rudder to coordinate turns is another result of the long wings. You've just experienced *adverse yaw*.

How Fast Is Fast?

As you glide away from your first thermal, you might wonder at what speed you should be flying. And, perhaps, for the first time since your grade school arithmetic teachers tried to interest you in simple arithmetic with time and distance problems (or tried to beat the same information into your skull!), the real-world answer to one of your questions will involve simple arithmetic computations. In a sense, the computations aren't necessary, just useful, for there are only three speeds at which most gliders are usually flown. You just flew at one of them in your thermalling climb. You flew at the speed which resulted in the least loss of altitude per unit of time. Also called *minimum sinking speed* (or *min sink*), it's a speed only slightly above the slowest speed the glider can fly and still support itself. Min sink speed is used all the times when climbing and is also useful when you're trying to stay aloft for as long as possible in the absence of lift.

But what if you were one mile out at sea on a windless morning, gliding to reach the beach? Shouldn't you be gliding at a speed which results in the flattest glide angle? Yes, indeed! This speed is the *maximum glide angle speed*, also called *max L/D*. As it turns out, max L/D speed is usually about 5 m.p.h. faster than min sink speed. You'll reach the ground in slightly less time than if you flew at min sink speed, but you'll glide farther.

So, you might reasonably ask, "Why not just fly at max L/D *between* thermals, and at min sink *in* thermals? Why fly at any other speed at all?"

Lots of reasons, not the least being that you simply want to. You can fly at any speed you wish, so long as you don't exceed the *maximum speed* of the glider, marked by a red line at the end of the yellow arc on the airspeed indicator. Probably your stomach, and definitely your pilot, won't allow you to do this on an introductory ride! But, except for aerobatic rides or at the end of the day when the sailplane pilot is burning off excess altitude before landing, whenever in a sailplane you're normally interested in flying as efficiently as possible. In thermals, efficiency is defined by how rapidly you climb, and min sink is obviously the speed to fly. Between thermals, efficiency can be defined as either the least amount of altitude lost in reaching the next thermal, or as the least amount of total time it takes you to reach the top of the next thermal. Counterintuitively, these require different speeds, speeds which also vary with the wind and the sink you encounter along the way. Only rarely are either of these speeds equal to max L/D, and only arithmetic can determine them for you. So, the third speed sailplanes normally fly isn't a fixed speed, but a constantly varying speed that depends on winds and what the air through which the plane glides is doing — rising or sinking — and how rapidly. Anyone who chooses to obtain a glider pilot's license eventually learns how to perform the straightforward calculations necessary to define precisely the most efficient speed to fly between thermals. Fortunately, until they do, choosing the wrong speed usually isn't terribly inefficient; most glider pilots waste far more time *not* going anywhere than they do *trying* to get somewhere once they decide to go! Dithering is far slower in a sailplane than choosing the wrong speed to fly.

On your introductory flight, it doesn't matter; any speed below about 80 m.p.h. won't make a bit of difference in how long you stay aloft on a decent soaring day. What speed should you fly between thermals? Any speed which allows you to have fun and enjoy the flight!

All Good Things Must End

Eventually, and regretfully, it will be time to hand the controls back to your pilot for landing. He'll fly an approach designed to ensure the glider always has more than sufficient altitude to reach the runway, regardless of how much sink you might encounter in the landing pattern. Preparing to land, you might be a bit concerned with the absence of an engine since, in a glider, you either get your landing approach right the first time or you crash! In more than 20 years of soaring, the author knows of only one glider that went around again on a botched approach, and that was while a thunderstorm was directly over the field causing wild turbulence, sheeting rain and dangerously strong lift. You won't go around.

Depending on how the airport you're flying from is laid out, perhaps influenced by other aerial traffic at the field, your landing pattern will consist of either three or four *legs* of a descending rectangle. This is called the *landing pattern* (see figure 1), and its purpose is to assist the pilot in judging the *angle of descent* so he can consistently land at a predetermined location on the runway. Commercial jets fly similar landing patterns, just much larger ones, due to their higher speeds. Landing an airplane is one of the trickiest things any pilot learns to do. Because our brains evolved in a two-dimensional world, it takes constant practice for us to become proficient in three dimensions. That's why, if you stop by any small airport to watch planes, you'll see some doing nothing but taking off, flying around the pattern and landing (known as doing *touch and goes*). In addition to allowing the intrepid aviators to commit aviation (which is fun!), it's a necessary safety practice.

Odds are you'll be landing the same direction you took off, which, if your pilot didn't mention it then, was into the wind. Taking off and landing into the prevailing breeze allows slower, safer takeoff and touchdown speeds, because the controls always have some air flowing past them even when the tire isn't rolling. Your pilot will probably fly directly over the center of the airport, perpendicular to the runway at about 800 feet above the ground, which will start to look, once again, like the place you're used to, instead of a slowly moving two-dimensional painting. For the first time, he'll check the *spoilers*; you'll be able to see and hear when they come out. You'll probably also feel a slight sinking sensation. This leg is called the *crosswind leg* of the pattern.

After flying a short distance beyond the runway, you'll turn onto the *downwind leg* of the pattern. Now you'll be flying with

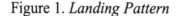

the breeze at your back, parallel to the runway, which you can easily watch out the side of the canopy. Somewhere along this leg, you'll notice the spoilers come into more or less continuous use as the pilot begins to bleed off his excess altitude. He'll do this slowly at first, because, until about the final few seconds of the approach, it's still possible to encounter strong sink. If you did, the pilot would first close the spoilers, gaining back in improved glide angle what the sink is costing him; if the sink persisted, he'd next simply turn toward the runway earlier, modifying the pattern to ensure the glider can always reach the runway.

On downwind, you'll fly beyond the end of the runway a short distance, then make another 90° turn until the glider is flying perpendicular to the runway again, but in the opposite direction from the crosswind leg. This is called the *base leg* and is the most critical portion of the landing pattern. This is because you're relatively close to the ground (and bad things to hit), and, for the first time, the pilot is getting to actually experience the existing winds close to the ground; surprisingly, they can sometimes be quite different than the winds aloft. If you're high, he might begin to use more spoilers; if low, he'll close spoilers and angle the base leg in toward the runway. Ideally, your glide path will be exactly in the center of the steepest and the shallowest *descent angles* of which your glider is capable.

Toward the end of base leg, for the first time you'll be able to anticipate another 90° turn, the turn onto the *final approach* leg, or *final* for short. No, pilots are not being ghoulish when they refer to being on their *final* approach. The fact is, every pilot sincerely hopes his current final approach is not his *final* final approach! By now

Figure 1. *Landing Pattern*

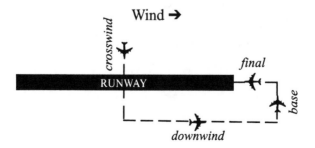

— on *your* final approach — it will be apparent you're sliding downhill toward the ground, and things will begin to slide by beneath you more and more rapidly. As on the takeoff, your brain will probably experience a slight sensory overload! On final approach, if there's a crosswind, you might sense the glider flying at an angle to the ground, nose pointed into the wind. This will keep the plane from drifting off the edge of the runway due to the crosswind. In any case, the pilot's goal is to touch down with the wheel parallel to the plane's direction of travel, so any *crab angle* due to a crosswind will be removed by the pilot before touchdown.

Just before you touch down, you might notice the nose of the glider rising slightly as the pilot *flares* to stop the plane's sink rate and bleed off the little extra safety speed he carried while flying the pattern. You'll feel a slight jolt when the plane contacts the ground, much more gently than even a light plane does, and nothing like the *thunk* of a commercial jet. As the pilot allows the plane to roll up to the area where you initially boarded, he might use slight *braking.* But with or without braking, he'll be able to hold the wings level with the stick until the plane halts. Then, one wing tip will slowly fall to the runway. With the wing on the ground like some wounded bird, you will be truly and unmistakably through flying!

To exit the sailplane, follow your pilot's lead. Depending on whether the plane is immediately scheduled, he may need your help pulling it back to the tiedowns. Whatever he advises you to do, you're encouraged to burn the experience into long-term memory! Talk about it. Relive it. Have someone take a picture of you, plane and pilot. Share your flight with friends and strangers on the observation deck. After all, sport soaring is simply that — a sport. Everyone who participates does so strictly for their individual perception of fun. Any advantages, accruing from increased self-confidence, improved judgment and new friendships, are free!

Baby Steps

Besides the obvious dangers associated with a sport capable of lofting a person to heights requiring supplemental oxygen, be forewarned: soaring can be addictive! For the psychologically hooked, the only known cure is another soaring flight.

So, if you're a person interested in taking an introductory ride, be prepared ahead of time to get hooked. One of the author's many unscientific surveys of the sport suggests the majority of soaring pilots have obtained licenses, not from any long-standing desire to be a pilot, but following a gift or whim ride. Clearly the experience *is* capable of setting a hook immediately and permanently. So, you should know, right up front, it'll cost around $2,000 to obtain a license from scratch. If cost is an insufficient deterrent, come along as we consider what you'll likely find, should you choose to explore the sport more deeply.

As a sport, soaring has much to offer potential participants. Like golf, it can be and is enjoyed by preteens to octogenarians. Like baseball, but far more so, it's a cerebral activity, rewarding those who most accurately perceive and correctly interpret nature's hints. Like many home hobbies, such as wood working, fly-tying, or painting, it demands precision and patience, yet it also rewards the timely bold stroke. And, of course, it's a fine excuse for outdoor socializing.

There are also some less-obvious aspects of the sport, which many participants find immensely rewarding. The adventurer or gardener in all of us might enjoy retrieving the pilot and glider who've landed in a plowed field many miles from home. It curiously blends elements of social and solitary experience, while attracting an eclectic group of job skills and personal interests, ranging from artists to scientists. You will meet interesting people in the sport.

Yet, somehow, the ethereal, unusual, visual and utterly unforgettable aspects of man-bird flight seem to tap a wellspring of sharing in all its participants, regardless of background. Perhaps it's a combination of the sheer unimaginableness of the experience by the uninterested (who never ask about it and are incapable of identifying with it), and because the sport isn't now and probably never will be a sport of the masses, that soaring pilots are so willing to share their experiences with anyone who does ask. Egos are almost always pleasantly absent at gliderports. But, whatever the reasons, you won't find secrecy at any gliderport. Regardless of skill level, any soaring pilot will happily try to help anyone who asks for it — a truly valuable resource for the beginner.

Finally, unlike power flying, no medical examination is required, merely the signing of a written statement to the effect that the signer has no known mental or physical defects which would impair their ability to safely pilot a sailplane. A person could lie about this, but why would one want to? Not only is it refreshing to be trusted by the government, but it is the pilot, himself, who would be put at the most risk.

Is soaring really so difficult, as I've already claimed? After all, the FAA has no lower-age limit for taking glider lessons, allowing youngsters to solo at age 14, and get their licenses at age 16. If a candidate can fit into the cockpit, reach the controls and find an instructor who feels they are mentally mature enough to exercise the good judgment soaring demands, soaring lessons can begin at any age. If the government thinks the sport is so easy, it surely must be! In fact, for the average individual (who starts with no previous experience and who can take two or three flights each day they train, and who can train no less infrequently than once each week), he or she can expect to solo a glider with somewhere around 25 to 35 flights, most of which will have been low-altitude, landing-pattern tows. Because people tend to forget some of what they've learned in previous lessons, during hiatuses of any longer than a week or so, expect it to take a bit longer if, like many people, your lessons must be more intermittent.

That hardly seems like much time, and it isn't.

But, know before you begin lessons, that soaring has a dirty secret, a skeleton in its closet. *You won't know how to soar by the time you've obtained your glider license!*

The ability to locate and effectively utilize the atmosphere's lift comes from reading, asking questions, dreaming and practice, not from your lessons. Odds are you'll do all these things during your instruction, of course, but most people obtain their licenses well before acquiring genuine soaring skills.

Prior to soloing, the bulk of instruction covers takeoff, towing, landing patterns and precision landings. Simultaneously covered are fundamental safety habits, like how to inspect the glider before every flight (*preflighting*), how to fly consistently coordinated turns, how to safely handle unplanned rope breaks, the development and maintenance of an effective scan for other aircraft, and the visual signals between tug and glider to alert each other of any unusual situation.

Arithmetic Can Be Your Friend

After solo, but before obtaining the actual license, the instructor reinforces things previously learned, introduces thermalling techniques and seeks to help the student develop the judgment which will prevent the student from ever accidentally damaging a glider by trying to stretch a glide back to an airport. Every glider pilot must learn to judge how far he can glide before entering a landing pattern. This is a skill needed for local or cross country flights, since a glider must never be allowed out of the range of a landable field. Here's where simple arithmetic is introduced to the student.

For example, even though the Schweizer 2-33 has a max L/D of 21:1 — which means in still air it can glide 21 miles for each mile of altitude it loses while gliding, no sane pilot ever counts on achieving the glider's *maximum* glide ratio, since sink will almost always be encountered along any glide. For planning purposes, the instructor will teach students training in this ship to assume a glide ratio of, say, 12:1. If the student is 3,000 feet above the pattern, how far from the field can he or she safely stray with this altitude? Rather than multiplying 3,000 feet times the assumed glide ratio of 12 then dividing by 5,280 feet per mile — a task few can do in their heads — a simple crutch is used.

The instrument that tells the student how high he is, the altimeter, reads in thousands of feet, so it's natural for the student to think of height in thousands of feet. Thus, if a glide *ratio* can be easily converted into a number expressed in *miles per thousand feet*, to determine how far one can go with a certain amount of altitude is simply done by multiplying how many thousands of feet of altitude a person has by this number. Fortunately, since a mile contains roughly 5,000 feet, ratios in multiples of five are simple to calculate. For example, a 25:1 glide ratio is approximately 5 miles per thousand feet, since 5 miles/thousand feet multiplied by 5 thousand feet/mile equals 25. Similarly, 4 miles per 1,000 feet equals a 20:1 glide ratio; 3

miles per 1,000 feet equals 15:1; and 2 miles per 1,000 equals 10:1.

Therefore, if a student has 3,000 feet to play with in a 2-33, if he assumes an achievable L/D of 12:1, so long as he stays 3,000 feet above the landing pattern, he can glide somewhere between 6 and 9 miles from the airport (3 times 2 miles per 1,000, and 3 times 3 miles per 1,000). With minor practice, performing this type of calculation is simple. The only other thing a student need then learn to do is estimate distances over the ground with reasonable accuracy, another skill easily learned, particularly in areas where roads are laid out on mile-long section lines. The method works for any glider of any performance. The pilot need only be able to estimate horizontal distances and assume a reasonable and conservative glide ratio. On an introductory flight in a twin Grob, the pilot typically assumes the Grob can achieve a 25:1 glide ratio, although the max L/D for the plane is much higher, around 35:1.

One method of reinforcing to the student that he or she, *not* the instructor, is pilot-in-command of the glider is the simple ploy of trying to lure the student beyond a comfortable glide slope back to the airport, typically under the guise of looking for lift. The instructor is trying to drive home the point that no matter how nice the lift *could* be, it's never good enough to put the glider (and pilot) at risk. Once the instructor is satisfied that the student both understands the importance of always being able to easily return to the airport and performs the calculations needed to confirm this condition is met, the door opens to the blossoming of the student's budding soaring skills. For, now, the student can fly, can keep safely within range of the airport and can, therefore, be safely sent solo to practice nascent skills.

At about this stage of instruction, the student will experience one of the biggest thrills any pilot can have, often exceeding even the excitement of soloing. He or she will make the transition to a single-seat glider. Very few pilots, outside the elite military fighter pilots, *ever* get to fly a single-seat airplane, and even they have the opportunity to fly two-seat versions of the planes beforehand. Only in gliders is it necessary to step directly into a plane, possibly having flight characteristics a person hasn't experienced before, and the person isn't human who won't experience sweaty palms, tightness in the chest, butterflies in the stomach and serious doubts prior to doing this! For, unlike two-seaters, your first attempts *must* be correct in a single seat glider, since there's no instructor to correct any minor mistakes you might make.

Even though it might seem obvious, your instructor wouldn't send you aloft in a single-seater unless you are truly ready. The realization is of small comfort when the time comes . . . as is the knowledge that thousands before you have safely done the same thing. The fact of the matter is that *you* have *not!* But you'll eventually strap in, motivated perhaps by the challenge or lured by the possibility of soaring on your own, and you'll do fine. You also won't touch the ground for a few days afterward!

Not All Fun and Games

For most students, actual soaring time begins to accumulate rapidly after they make the transition to single-seaters. They've crossed another of several learning plateaus which normally frustrate all students and are once again on a rewarding, exciting ascent toward a higher plane of knowledge. You'll be introduced to various *achievement badges* now within reach of your skills. First pursued are usually *height- and duration-based badges*. Later, *distance badges* might be pursued, but, at this stage of your experience, the thought of ever soaring 311 miles to qualify for the *diamond distance badge* will seem impossible.

For now, you'll concentrate on honing the skills so patiently introduced by your instructor and so painstakingly layered within your brain. You are preparing to take the written and the flight tests which must be passed before the Feds will issue you the piece of paper telling the world *you* are a glider pilot.

The written test covers two primary topics: glider safety and glider-related FARs (Federal Aviation Regulations). Since part of your instruction will have been the purchase of several training books, by the time you're ready to take the written, it will seem less like some unimaginable hurdle than just another affirmation of what you already know. Few people have trouble with it, save those who know everything before they begin and whose wake-up call is failing the test!

The flying test will be different, no matter how much your instructor attempts to put it in perspective; he might even downplay it, depending on your psychological makeup. Not to worry. *You'll* think it's a big deal — and it is. For when your instructor signs your logbook, attesting to the belief you're ready for the flight test, he or she is putting their instructing skills on the line almost as much as you'll be putting to the test your new flying skills. The *FAA Examiner*, or *FAA Designee* (a private individual the FAA allows to act in government capacity), rightfully expects the two of you to have reached a certain level of safety and competency, which only *you* can demonstrate to him during the 1 to 3 flights you'll typically make. Once again, it'll be sweaty-palms time.

The flight test actually consists of two parts, the first of which is an *oral evaluation*. Expect the examiner to verbally cover in detail those areas in which your written test scores displayed weakness. It might help to know that, even though the examiner has the power to fail you, deep down he really wants you to pass, since he's already as much of a soaring nut as you're becoming. Still, there *are* some things which will guarantee failure on your part.

Since the oral will be given prior to the flight test, any evidence that you haven't boned up on your weak written test areas will definitely make a negative impression on the examiner. Presuming you pass the oral (most people do), it'll be time to go flying!

Just as with your instruction, bear in mind that, even

though the examiner has far more experience than you, *you* are *pilot in command (PIC)* of your test flights, and, as such, he expects you to exercise the sensible judgments of a PIC. Sure, he'll probably try to lure or distract you away from the field to get you to make a low approach — don't let him. He can't *order* you to do anything you think is unsafe, he can merely suggest. If you can avoid succumbing to this sort of psychological error, the only other way to fail the flight test is to make any of several mechanical mistakes.

So long as you don't inadvertently stall while thermalling or while making the slow turns he'll ask you to, or you don't forget to check the wind prior to landing (and possibly commit the sin of landing downwind), or you don't land too far away from your aiming point, you'll likely pass the flight test. Still, if you do fail for any reason or combination of reasons, it isn't the end of the world. After a little more instruction and practice, you can make another appointment with the examiner.

Odds are, though, you'll do just fine, and, after some simple paperwork following the test — you *are* dealing with the federal government, after all — you'll walk away with a big grin and a *temporary Private Pilot's License, Glider Rating*. The mailman will deliver your permanent one in a month or so.

With the new license will accrue one significant new privilege: you can now take family and friends for glider rides! You can't take people for profit, but you *can* share expenses. Additionally, you can legally fly any single-seater you choose to; as a student, you needed your instructor's endorsement in your logbook for flight in any single-seater. That thought, alone, will probably help you keep your newly-acquired certificate in perspective! The truth is, you're not god's gift to the piloting kingdom and you might not even be the best newly-licensed pilot on that field that day! What you really hold in your happy hands is *a license to learn.*

The question you'll soon be asking yourself is, "Learn what?" In the meantime, have fun!

Chapter Five

Beyond the Flagpole

Those things which attract a person to soaring often aren't what maintain their interest in the long run. Dreams long held and strongly imagined can vanish to nothingness once accomplished; difficult challenges can lose significance with mastery. In this sense, soaring is no different from any other experience and skill. Not every flight can hope to match the thrill of one's first ride in a sailplane.

As eloquently demonstrated in this generations's experience by mankind's tentative challenge of the outer space frontier, repetition is an anesthetic to the most dramatic of events, and soaring isn't immune. But the one thing nature unfailingly provides soaring, even before humans add their own diversionary twists, is variety. Indeed a spice to life, it's this endless variety of experiences and challenges, open to all soaring pilots, which serves to snare the unwary and the jaded in surprising ways. Beyond every mastered skill, every learning plateau, are still more challenges, some quite unimaginable, if not incomprehensible, until reinforced by actual experience.

The course one charts through soaring's web is unique simply because individuals are unique. For some, the thrill of their first flight evolves to immersion in aerobatics; except for the physical limitations imposed by their long wings and the absence of an engine, gliders are capable of most of the same aerobatic maneuvers as powerplanes. Others discover a previously unsuspected desire and talent as airborne ambassadors, perhaps by giving rides, perhaps by providing formal instruction. Natural human competitiveness finds acceptable outlets in soaring contests, ranging from local to regional to national, and even to international world championships, which are exactly and truly that, not an overblown expression of some promotional hack. Soaring world champions become what they are, not in pursuit of economic return, but for other, more personal reasons. A person would be better off to plant a garden than to become a soaring champion, if eating well is part of their motivation for seeking fame!

Without exaggeration, soaring combines beauty, grace, personal challenges, group competition and much more, rewarding its practitioners with intangibles like improved self-esteem and judgment, peer respect and self-confidence. Access to all these things results from knowledge and piloting skill. Unless a pilot can make his craft climb when he needs to, frustration will prevail. Come explore what you can find beyond cloudbase.

Lift!

It isn't long before anyone interested in soaring learns of the "Big Three" . . . types of lift that is. Thermal, ridge lift, and waves. No book about the sport is complete without their mention!

Thermals are convective, direct children of the sun. Probably their most commonly recognized forms are summer thunderstorms. To the sailplane pilot, thunderstorms are the ultimately overdeveloped transmutation of your garden-variety, fair-weather thermal. Both result from uneven solar heating of the earth's surface, which, in turn, heats the air above unevenly, causing the heated air to rise.

Before common knowledge of another of the "Big Three",
sailplane pilots routinely utilized the daunting updrafts
within growing cumulonimbus thunderstorm clouds as a
means of attaining great heights. Although the practice remains legal today with the inclusion of some blind flying
instruments and radios, few people attempt it (outside of
atmospheric research scientists). There are less exciting
ways to gain extreme height! Using only convective lift
beneath clouds' bases, the world record thermal flight distance is 907.2 miles, from the shores of the Baltic Sea, in
northern Germany, to the Pyrenees, separating France from
Spain.

Ridge lift is what most people ignorant about soaring
probably have in mind when they inevitably ask, after your
glider has landed in their field, "What happened, did the
wind quit?" For anyone can imagine a wind blowing over a
ridge rising and generating lift. Soaring actually got its
start utilizing ridge lift, initially with the Wright brothers,
then more permanently in Germany following World War
I. Not until the late 1920s were thermals discovered, used,
and variometers ultimately designed to make their use
practical for all soaring pilots. Today, the majority of the
world's longest sailplane flights have used ridge lift to fly
out and back along the Alleghenies, including the world's
first flight to exceed 1,000 miles.

Toward the end of the 1930s, *waves* were discovered,
but the phenomenon wasn't studied and understood until
the early 1950s. The Sierra Wave Project was funded by
the U.S. Air Force, which was concerned about the potential of waves to damage high flying bombers. Although the
study utilized a four-engined, B-50 bomber among other
planes, the primary research vehicles were planes designed
and built for just such high-altitude work — sport sailplanes flown by private glider pilots, not professional military pilots! Even today, except within the soaring community, atmospheric waves are little-understood phenomena
to be assiduously avoided. To sailplane pilots, they're a
magical elevator to the sky, of ineffable tranquility and

smoothness, bordered below with eye-popping turbulence.

The atmosphere is a fluid, similar to water in some ways, and just as a standing ripple will form downstream of a rock in a flowing stream, so will atmospheric ripples form downstream of hills. But atmospheric ripples have one major difference from aquatic ripples; they rebound to heights far greater than the obstruction generating them. Today, it's known that atmospheric waves (also called *lee waves*, or most commonly, just *waves*) can reach heights exceeding 100,000 feet! The world record height for gliders is 49,009 feet, achieved in California. It won't likely be exceeded until someone equips a sailplane with a pressure suit, for even breathing oxygen under pressure through a special mask is insufficient protection against the extremely low pressures of such altitudes.

Interestingly, the world's longest sailplane flight, exceeding 1,250 miles, used wave lift almost exclusively. The pilot fought bitter cold, clouds, poor visibility, and the sea, along the way. He traversed nearly the complete length of New Zealand's North and South Islands, twice, including two crossings of Cook Strait!

These three phenomena (thermals, ridge lift and waves) are described in more detail in a subsequent chapter. For current purposes, know that, although the "Big Three" are surely the most common forms of lift, they're far from the only types.

Whenever streams of air, moving different directions or of different densities, collide, *shear lift* happens. In certain areas of the country, shears provide many soaring opportunities, particularly in the Mojave Desert region of California and near the shores of large lakes and oceans. Not yet well understood, another form of shear lift from converging air masses is fairly commonly used by more experienced pilots to fly cross country in certain areas of the mountain west.

Also common in mountainous terrain is a form of hybrid lift yet to be given an accepted name. If you've ever

seen smoke from a large fire rising while blowing downwind, you can imagine this turbulent, disorganized lift,
typically found on the downwind slopes of sun-soaked, continuous ridge lines. Although the lifting mechanism is unquestionably a combination of thermal activity and wind,
the means the glider pilot uses to effectively utilize the
resulting ragged lift differs from the techniques used when
in thermals or ridge lift.

Challenges and Recognition

As soaring skills accumulate, it isn't long before pilots
seek the three legs of the *Silver Badge*. The *Silver Altitude
leg* requires a height gain above any previous low point
(after release from the towplane of course!) of 1,000 meters
(3281 feet). The *Silver Distance leg* requires a cross country flight of 50 kilometers (31.1 miles). The *Silver Duration leg* requires a soaring flight of five hours. While a person can qualify for all badge legs on a single flight, many
people choose to go after them one leg at a time. More commonly, acquiring them one by one happens simply because
the skills needed for each differ significantly.

By simply carrying aloft a *barograph* (a recording altimeter available at any soaring site), proof these goals have
been met is readily attained. Probably the first leg most
new pilots achieve is Silver Altitude, followed by Silver Duration. It's during their duration flight that the first hint
of boredom typically rears its disturbing head, but it is soon
dispelled by the thought of actually gliding beyond reach
of the airport. (*Gulp!*)

No one will force you to fly cross country in a sailplane, but for those who continue with the sport (even if
they choose not to often do it), many don't feel comfortable
in their local flying until acquiring the skills making cross
country flight safely possible. In a nutshell, the key to safe,
if not low-stress, cross-country flight is learning how to se-
lect good fields from the glider — fields you've never seen
before. From prior training, the pilot already knows how

to do everything else needed to land safely.

Because of their light weight and low landing speeds, gliders are quite capable of safely landing away from paved airports, and the very nature of the sport practically demands its practitioners gain this skill. For, sooner or later, on a local flight, developing weather, unpredictable winds or the pursuit of expanded skills will force you to the ground short of the field. Learning how to safely do this is surprisingly easy, in a technical sense, but awesomely difficult for most, in a psychological sense. But if there is a single key to opening the door to lifelong interest in soaring, learning how to make off-field landings is it.

With this weapon in a soaring pilot's arsenal, he can literally fly wherever and whenever he wants, limited only by weather, the performance of his ship and personal capabilities. Flagpole sitting atop thermals near the local airport? Never again!

Having plunked a glider onto some stranger's field, it's removed on (often *in*) a specially designed trailer, for all gliders are designed for rapid and easy wing removal. Most privately owned gliders are actually stored in their trailers and assembled for each flight. With practice, assembly can be performed in under 10 minutes; disassembly typically is slightly faster. With typical single-seat glider weights — sans pilot — of 500 to 600 pounds, each wing weighs around 125 to 170 pounds, with most of the weight at the root end of the wing. With the assistance of some simple, clever devices such as a fuselage dolly and a wing stand, most gliders can be easily rigged and de-rigged by two people.

At almost every gliderport in the land, available to assist the new soaring pilot along the path to soaring freedom, will be a soaring club or collection of private owners. The combination of capital costs of the gliders themselves, and life's other interests and demands, makes joint ownership of gliders a natural consequence, hence the common existence of soaring clubs and partnerships. Within these organizations will always be found a wide range of soaring skills. Additionally, for reasons of fun and encouraging continuing development of flight skills, most clubs regularly sponsor spot landing contests, "flour bombing" contests, cross country seminars and other activities, including postflying barbecues. Sooner or later, opportunities to retrieve outlanded pilots provide the crew a free meal, sight-seeing to some remarkable places (The author has helped retrieve a glider and pilot from a wilderness area — a helicopter and horses were involved!), the chance to meet new people and — not least — the chance to interrogate the intrepid pilot. All of this wonderfully de-mystifies the new sailplane pilot's naturally preexisting fears of flying cross country and the inevitable outlandings.

Despite the skill required to effectively soar, most principles of flight are simply stated, including cross-country flight. Flying is really safe so long as you don't hit anything! Don't want to hit gopher holes or rocks? Land in plowed and harrowed fields. Don't want to hit fences or trees? Pick fields without any, or pick large fields. And of course, don't land in fields with crops or critters. Paradoxically, whenever flying cross country in a sailplane, it can often be safer to land in a field than at a small airport, because — although undeniably smooth — paved airports are designed for powerplanes with their short wings, and often contain hidden dangers to gliders, such as runway lights and tall grass adjacent to the runway.

None of this is enough to frighten anyone genuinely interested in maximizing personal soaring opportunities, of course. All of it quite naturally becomes just more fun stuff to learn and ultimately apply. School in the sky.

As for those times when your goals are limited strictly to flying locally (which might also include hopping around a course of local airports), what is there to maintain continuing interest? One item is practicing precision flight skills, more or less in formation! Many gliders, particularly trainers and lower-performance single seaters, spend well over half their lives flying within a few miles per hour of stalling speed — thermalling. After all, height is the beginning glider pilot's best insurance against landing. Not surprisingly, then, precision flying becomes a way of life for glider pilots. And, since one glider thermalling attracts more like a dump attracts seagulls, it isn't long before the neophyte finds other gliders horning in on *his* lift! Learning how to safely and efficiently thermal with other gliders becomes an early challenge. Every new soaring pilot disbelieves when told the clunky 2-33 and its performance cousin, the single seat Schweizer 1-26, can out climb any other glider around; new pilots always mistakenly equate good gliding performance with good climbing performance. But real masters of the sport are invariably superb climbers, a skill they first honed in basic training ships and work ceaselessly to improve.

Upon leaving a thermal, another distinction between tyro and tiger appears. Quite commonly, the beginner glides out some short distance, encountering only the normal sink around a thermal's periphery, before turning tail and slinking back to the previous thermal — all too often only to find it dying, because thermals routinely have lives measured in minutes. The experienced glider pilot, meanwhile, continues gliding along until encountering the next thermal, several miles away. And the beginner? Even if his thermal is still cooking, he returns to it with very little altitude loss, and so ends up spending the bulk of his time "climbing" at the very top of the same thermal, until it eventually *does* quit.

Flying in such a manner is the main reason beginners are often mystified to learn, at the conclusion of their flight, that the experienced pilots have a completely different picture of the day than theirs. Spending most of your time thermalling near thermal tops results in short climbs and in ragged and bumpy lift; the top of the thermal is capped by warmer air aloft, literally causing the thermal's rising air to bump into a wall, forcing it to expand horizontally before it can begin sinking. Hence, the bumps and weak lift. Had the beginner allowed himself to start his climb from a lower altitude, he'd have found stronger, steadier lift, rising for thousands of feet.

Learning to have faith in the atmosphere and learning to judge the spacing of thermals can be quite challenging.

Eventually, typically after a year or so of normal flight activity, the raw beginner comes to realize he or she is spending less time worrying about climbing and more time enjoying the plane's immediate surroundings. Without noticing exactly when, they've begun to spontaneously explore the sky, trying to climb the sides of cumulus clouds or venturing closer to the site's ridge or seeking entry to a wave. Without telling anyone, for misplaced fear of being laughed at, they attempt to follow more experienced pilots. They can't keep up with them, naturally. But with each flight, more confidence is gained. The rubber band pulling them inexorably back to the home airport stretches more and more, until finally it snaps. The new pilot is, at last, undeniably beyond direct gliding distance to the home airport. They are flying cross country. Oddly, beginners often report they relax and begin flying much better once this happens!

Usually, about this time, they begin trying for their *Gold Badge*, which requires a soaring height gain of 3,000 meters (9,843 feet), and a distance flight of 300 kilometers (186.4 miles). The distance sounds much longer than it is, since on a moderately good day in a medium-performance sailplane, only 15 thermals might be needed (a smaller number than the pilot likely worked on his first, five-hour flight). Nevertheless, even if flown as a triangle or an out and return course rather than straight out distance, it's mostly out of direct gliding distance from home, a real challenge!

The first time the author flew the distance was as a competitor in a local contest. Beleaguered with a marginally road-worthy trailer at the time and flying in thunderstorm shadows for much of the distance, it took him nearly six hours and he was — as usual — one of the slowest finishers. But he finished in the top third, because most pilots failed to make it around the triangular course. He had a blast, too, landing tired, exhilarated, happy to be back and ready to do it again.

Pilots who secure a Gold Badge inevitably stalk the even tougher *Diamond Badge*, which requires a 5,000 meter (16,404 feet) height gain, and two distance flights, one of 500 kilometers (310.7 miles), and another to a pre-declared goal of 300 kilometers (186.4 miles).

With ever-increasing glider performance and pilots' soaring knowledge over the years, additional — even more challenging — goals are coming into recognition. But, for most, pursuing Silver, Gold and Diamond badges will provide challenge enough in your initial years!

Chapter Six

In the Beginning

Soaring aloft, enjoying the spectacle to be had immersed enginelessly in nature's grand aerial ocean, cosseted in the upholstered comfort of a tandem-seated fiberglass sailplane on one's first sailplane ride, most people's thoughts are far from how the ride they're enjoying is possible. For most, their first soaring ride is an end in itself, perhaps the culmination of a childhood of dreams, the excitement of fulfilling a whim, the sharing of a new experience. For two brothers from Dayton, Ohio, gliding was a means to an end.

Little-known today, in the world-changing repercussions of the Wright brothers' invention of powered flight, is their contribution to the creation of an entirely different arena of flight. In fact, this separate arena came into existence well over a year before December 17, 1903, the date on which they first achieved controlled, powered flight. For Wilbur and Orville were also the first humans to achieve truly controlled *gliding* flight and, ultimately, controlled *soaring* flight. From their efforts directly sprang today's sport of soaring.

Technically, soaring differs from gliding in that to achieve *soaring flight* the pilot must climb higher than his release altitude or must remain aloft longer than his craft would otherwise be capable without the help of rising air currents. In the early days, this distinction contained much more significance than it does today, when soaring is the norm. In the ninety-plus years since the Wrights changed the world, the sport of soaring has progressed no less remarkably than has powered flight, until, today, soaring flights exceeding 1,000 miles have been made in both the United States and New Zealand. While flying a two-seater, two French brothers recently soared 859.4 miles across southern France, south along Spain's east coast and on across the Mediterranean Sea to land in Morocco over 13 hours later – farther than anyone else has ever flown a multi-place sailplane.

The advances in soaring flight have come largely on three fronts: scientific knowledge of the atmosphere, increased knowledge of aerodynamics and improved structural technology. The first advance has resulted in better pilots, while the latter two have resulted in astoundingly advanced sailplanes. Most sailplanes you will see today at any gliderport in the United States are but distant cousins of the bi-winged, fabric-covered, wooden gliders of 1901 and 1902, with which the brothers Wright taught themselves to fly. Let's explore this evolution.

To understand how today's sport soaring has come to be, we can trace backward along the history of powered aircraft development to the Wright brothers. While others glided ungainly (and deadly) contraptions before the Wrights' experiments began (most prominently Otto Lilienthal in Germany), this path of aeronautical development is more closely related to the sport of hang gliding today than it is to soaring. Of the many intellectually giant leaps the Wrights made, perhaps their largest was being the first to realize that man's dreams of flight had less to do with the creation of a lifting craft than it did the *control* of that craft once it lifted itself and its pilot into the air. Thus, their first serious aeronautical experiments utilized controllable bi-winged kites; their goal was to learn how to make them climb on command, descend, go to the right, go to the left. Not until spending the better part of a summer convincing themselves they knew enough to continue did they take the next step, the inevitably dangerous one of risking their lives by putting their theories to the test . . . the *human* flight test.

They built a larger, bi-winged kite, one capable — according to their calculations — of lifting their body weight with a generous safety margin. While initially flying it tethered, they ultimately learned the basics of taking off this glider, flying it in a controlled straight line and safely landing it. It took them another year and a number of close calls before they understood how to safely control it in a turn. By their third summer of glide tests, they knew their sole, remaining step was to add an engine. Remarkably, so knowledgeable had they become, that they actually considered the addition of an engine a relatively trivial step, despite the fact they had to design and build the engine themselves! Part of the reason for their confidence lay in the many glides they'd made along the dunes of Kitty Hawk the summer of 1902 — more than 1,000 of them. While most flights were quite short, and their total flight time as pilots was probably less than 5 hours, this time likely vastly exceeded the flight experience of all other would-be pilots in human history *combined*, and 1902 was the year they became *pilots*.

In 1903, on December 17, with mankind's first engine-powered takeoff, controlled flight and landing, they essentially ended their gliding experiments for the next eight years.

With powered, controlled flight now a reality, simple glides no longer held appeal for anyone. Nevertheless, in 1911 — again on the dunes of North Carolina — Orville set a world record for duration in one of their gliders (9 minutes and 45 seconds). He later claimed he did it for the sheer fun of it, but the historical record is cloudy on his true motivation. Regardless, this marked the first true soaring flight ever made. Using 40 m.p.h. winds sweeping against the North Carolina sand dunes, Orville, at one point, soared to a height of more than 50 feet above the top of the dunes. Man's first soaring flight used what we today call ridge lift; it also demonstrated the distinction between soaring flight and gliding flight. All planes are capable of gliding flight, but only specially designed craft have the low sink rates which enable them to routinely gain altitude — to *soar* — on their glides. If this distinction is a source of concern to the reader, lest s/he exhibit ignorance by using improper terminology in the presence of sailplanes and those who fly them, don't worry. In the U.S., the terms are used interchangeably — routinely so by participants in the sport. Even airports which cater primarily to soaring operations are called *gliderports*, not soaringports or sailplaneports. The distinction becomes important only in the context of an individual flight.

The 1911 expedition was the Wright's last to Kitty Hawk and Kill Devil Hills, and soaring languished until after The Great War. The political peace, imposed in 1919 by the victors, shaped future societies at all levels, including unpowered flight. In their zeal to ensure Germany could never again make war on her neighbors after this "war to end all wars," Germany was stripped of her air force, and the design of powered aircraft in Germany was forbidden for several years. Banning powered flight is not the same thing as banning *dreams* of flight, however, and, not surprisingly, an almost immediate interest in gliding flight developed in postwar Germany.

The first informal postwar glider meet occurred in 1919 on the Wasserkuppe Hills in central Germany. Two years later, the then-formal meet had attracted nearly 50 gliders, including the soon to-be-famous *Blaue Maus* (Blue Mouse) monoplane glider. The *Blaue Maus* incorporated many of the features now considered standard on sailplanes, including long span wings, neatly faired landing gear and enclosed fuselage (but not pilot). With designer/builder/graduate student (and eventually Dr.) Wolfgang

Klemperer at the controls, the *Blaue Maus* broke Orville's duration record by remaining aloft for 13 minutes. Before the meet was over, two other pilots in two different planes had soared 15 minutes and 21 minutes. Curiously, the 21-minute flight was made in one of the cruder airplanes at the meet, suggesting there was much for would-be sailplane pilots to learn about the atmosphere!

By 1922, national glider meets were also held in Great Britain and France, as well as Germany. An American group from the Massachusetts Institute of Technology (MIT) took a glider of their own design to the French and German meets. Eddie Allen from MIT attended all three meets, subsequently writing America's first comprehensive report on soaring. His and the ship's performance in the meet bespoke of the largest problem facing all pioneers in the sport: lack of experience. While trying to gain additional experience after the conclusion of the meet, he lost control of the ship in the gusty conditions prevailing at the Wasserkuppe and cracked it up. As with many of these early incidents, the proximity of the ground, combined with the slow flying speed of the plane, ensured Eddie's survival with little more than bruised pride. The plane, though, was written off.

In the French meet, which was the first to be held that year, the longest flight was but three minutes long. By the end of the next meet, the German one, the duration record had been raised to 3 hours and 10 minutes. Not long afterward at the English meet, the record was again raised, to 3 hours and 20 minutes. All of these flights were in ridge lift, air deflected up and over slopes perpendicular to the prevailing wind.

Not until 1929, in the U.S., was an American to exceed Orville Wright's duration record. In another ridge lift flight, this time along Cape Cod's sand dunes, Ralph Barnaby soared for 15 minutes. He did so as a student of the first soaring school ever set up in the United States. A year earlier, the chief pilot of the school had been the first foreign national to exceed Orville's time in the U.S. by remaining aloft at the school site for more than four hours, so Barnaby was learning from some of the world's best. The school's instructors had all honed their skills in Germany. (Today, while on an individual basis, U.S. pilots have demonstrated world record-setting and world championship-winning performances since the 1950s, taken as a whole, German sailplane technology, level of pilot activity and overall pilot skills have remained arguably the best in the world since that first informal 1919 meet.)

By current standards, the level of development of these early gliders was primitive, the launches labor intensive and the vast majority of the flights short. Danger was a constant companion. Launching from slopes meant the participants were completely dependent on the wind coming from the proper direction if there was to be any hope at all of soaring flight. But whether launched down the slope into a wind for soaring flights or launched down a windless slope for basic flight training, launches and retrieves were wonders of human coordination and effort. The center of a long, elastic band was attached to an open hook mounted below the nose of the glider, which itself was either staked by the tail to the ground or had a couple of heavy, strong, brave people holding on to the leading edge of the vertical stabilizer. The glider was positioned at the crest of the slope, facing the valley below. Two groups of enthusiastic people grabbed hold of either end of the elastic band, and — making certain they were beyond the wingtips of the glider — in a form of aeronautical tug of war, set out down slope as fast as both groups could coordinate their trots, aided by helpful commands from the open cockpit of, "Walk. Trot. Run!" As the tension in the elastic band (and the cockpit!) increased, they naturally slowed down — a sight watched closely by the glider pilot who, at what he deemed the propitious moment, released the tail stake or else shouted for the tail to be released. The glider then surged forward across the grass, pulled by the energy stored in the elastic, whizzed by the launch crews now tumbled about in two heaps, all their hopes riding with the pilot. If they were lucky, they got to laugh and recover their breaths a bit before being pressed into retrieving the glider, which had landed all too soon at the bottom of the slope. At first, humans and horses dragged the gliders back up the slopes until the participants could afford to use another newfangled invention — cars.

Human-powered launches were only possible due to the extremely slow flying speeds of the early gliders. Humans are not capable of storing large quantities of energy in the elastic bands (which, back then, were called *shock* cords; today we'd call them *bungee* cords). Bungee-launching a modern sailplane would likely be an exercise in futility in all but the strongest of winds, because of the increased weights and flying speeds of modern craft.

But while ground launches were work, they were also a labor of love. The level of shared excitement at these early glider launches might be compared to a modern day equivalent, a team sport at the Olympics. Participants were literally making history and advancing the state of the art, and most of them were probably well aware of those facts. Wars have been started with less motivation. Contributing to the excitement were the open cockpits of the sailplanes; ground crew and pilot could communicate easily as the pilot flew back and forth along the slope. Danger was ever present, as illustrated by Ralph Barnaby's record-setting 15 minute flight.

Two gliders were disassembled and hauled across a local feature, known as Corn Hill, to the dunes facing the water at Cape Cod. The original plan was for Barnaby to fly the higher-performance glider in an attempt to soar long enough to qualify for an achievement certificate. He needed five minutes! As that glider had not been flown since its arrival from Germany, a more experienced German pilot from the school decided to make a check flight before Barnaby's flight, for safety's sake. On his bungee launch, he zoomed up too steeply, stalled and did one turn of a spin before crashing to the beach below. That little setback didn't deter Barnaby or the rest of the crew. Once the determination was made that the school pilot's most serious injury was one to his pride, Barnaby climbed into the much-lower-performance training glider, successfully launched, and, in the good breeze blowing over the brow of the dunes, he cruised back and forth, sometimes 50 feet above the crest. In Ralph's own words, "When the necessary five minutes had been completed, I was enjoying it so much that I decided to keep going. It was then that I recalled Orville Wright's Nineteen-eleven soaring flight of nine minutes forty-five seconds, and decided, 'Why not?'! With fifteen minutes under my belt, I finally heeded Herr Knott's pleading and landed."

Herr Knott, of course, was the unfortunate pilot who had minutes earlier crashed the high-performance glider, and who no doubt had been shouting nearly 10 minutes for Barnaby to land!

Even before the sport of soaring was gaining a foothold in the United States, dozens of clubs in Germany were training hundreds of enthusiasts. Their interests in the sport were maintained by the rapid-fire discoveries being made as soaring skills and pilots' knowledge of the atmosphere burgeoned. In a burst of knowledge, probably more rapid than the soaring world has seen since, between 1926 (when it was proved soaring was not entirely a fair-weather sport) and the time of Barnaby's flight, German soaring pilots were continuously breaking records. In 1926, the first soaring flight in hail and rain was made. That same year, another pilot was accidentally sucked up into a thunderstorm cloud to a height never before reached by a sailplane; the pilot used the altitude to glide more than 30 miles before landing. In 1928, the existence of thermals was proven at the Wasserkuppe when Robert Kronfeld, a young Austrian, was the first to make use of information meteorologists had known for some time — that updrafts existed beneath cumulus clouds.

Launching from the ridge, he slope-soared until a cloud began to form above the line of hills, positioned himself on a line extending into the wind from the cloud's location, encountered the rising air which formed the cloud and climbed 1,400 feet. He then glided to a nearby town on another slope, where he waited again in the slope winds until he could make contact with other clouds and, by their help, return to his starting point. By 1929, what was then called *cloud soaring* became common practice, and less than a month before Ralph Barnaby's record-setting slope-soaring flight in the U.S., Kronfeld made a second great contribution to the technique of motorless flight. Launching from the Wasserkuppe on a day when thunderstorms were expected, he intentionally utilized the lift below and ahead of their movement to soar a record 85.5 miles and climb a record 7,525 feet. Although the existing duration record exceeded 12 hours, the allure of ridge soaring, alone, probably would not have been strong enough to sustain people's continuing interest in the sport. After Kronfeld's flight, ridge-soaring pilots sensed an invisible pathway to extended freedom from the geographic trap of the ridges; the sport forever changed.

People sought ways of identifying these thermals, of knowing when they were near or in one. For, despite the open cockpits most sailplanes still had, a human's ability to sense the slightly warmer air of a thermal was woefully insufficient. In the early 1930s, encountering and utilizing one of these marvelous thermals was largely a matter of luck. The desire to know when one was in a thermal led directly to the invention of the variometer. While unable to *see* thermals not yet encountered, the variometer did show when the sailplane was rising or sinking. When ridge soaring, that wasn't important, since the ridge itself served as the pilot's altimeter and variometer. He could *see* when he was rising or descending. But once he rose several hundred feet above the crest of his hill, his eyes lost the sensitivity required to tell if the presence of a thermal was continuing to loft him skyward. Something else was needed. In various forms, that "something else" remains the variometer to this day, for, with the possible exception of the night-vision goggles developed for military helicopter pilots, man has still not developed an instrument capable of seeing thermals before the glider pilot reaches them. Soaring flight remains much more an art than a science.

The variometer unleashed another knowledge explosion. The ridge was man's doorway to soaring flight, the thermal his stairway to the skies, the variometer his roadmap to the horizon. After more than a decade, pilots were truly freed from the geographical trap of the ridges.

It wasn't long before the dangers associated with this new freedom became all too apparent. Eager pilots, their planes carrying barographs — recording altimeters — began to climb into clouds, the more sensible ones also carrying blind-flying instruments. But all too often, the end result was a tangle of wreckage falling from the cloud, carrying the hapless pilot to his death. Soon, people knew there was danger beyond the obvious one of losing control in the cloud because of the impossibility of seeing a reference horizon. Blind-flying instruments, parachutes and pilot skill all proved insufficient to prevent the breakup of planes and the deaths of pilots. The exploration of clouds in sailplanes gradually changed from the thrill of discovery to the precision of science. It had to. Still, in the 1930s, it was learned that turbulence and altitude — and perhaps cold — were the killers.

The largest problem was in thunderstorms, not fair-weather cumulus clouds. As storms built, the heat rushing into them created cloud towers we now know can exceed 50,000 feet. But meteorologists in the 1930s lacked knowledge of the massive power contained in thunderstorms. Turbulence within them could — and still can — rip planes apart, sometimes even before the pilot lost control and the wings shed in the ensuing dive. Pilots went so high they lost consciousness from lack of oxygen; with no hand at the controls, the planes inevitably fell into a spiralling dive which overstressed the wings. Also, as pilots went higher, the air temperature decreased. Below the clouds the temperature drops 5.5°F for every thousand feet gained. Inside the clouds, it decreases more slowly, only 3.2°F per thousand feet. So, from a ground temperature of 80°F at takeoff to 12,000 feet, it can easily drop to below freezing. In the open-cockpit gliders of that day, the wind chill alone was formidable, notwithstanding the possible rain, lightning and hail likely to be inside mature thunderstorms. Heavy loads of ice, accumulated in thunderheads, weighted down gliders and destroyed the flow over the wings needed to create lift; the man-made ice cubes crashed.

In the mid-1930s, led by the Germans, sailplane pilots gradually learned the true nature of the different types of convective clouds, and they learned how to use them for cross-country soaring flights without inadvertently putting their lives at risk. Pilots and planes improved. With the proper instruments and the experience to use them, cloud flying became a common practice in the humid and cloud-laden skies of Europe. This was much less so in the United States, much of which is so dry there is little advantage to be gained from soaring inside clouds. Sailplanes were designed to new — stronger — standards as a result of what was learned. Enclosed cockpits began to appear, their need stemming both from pilot comfort and the quest for better sailplane performance. For with cross-country flight now a real possibility, it became increasingly important for gliders to have low sink rates in order to most effectively utilize thermal lift. Decreasing the aerodynamic turbulence and drag of an open cockpit was an obvious step in the right direction. Longer wings was another result.

While the designers struggled to invent the best types of sailplanes for exploiting what was known about the atmosphere, the pilots found that increased understanding of the air through which they glided also led to improved soaring skills. It was one thing to leave the top of a thermal then glide blindly until you blundered into another; it was quite another to head directly for where your knowledge of the earth and the atmosphere suggested the next one would be. Understanding the nature of this new lift, so recently discovered, became every soaring pilot's goal.

Chapter Seven

The Sport Today

In time, pilots came to understand more fully that the sun is what makes all soaring flight possible. In this sense, gliders aren't engineless, they have the biggest engine in the solar system — the sun! Energy from the sun's atomic furnace constantly bombards the earth. Of the energy reaching our planet, 42% of it is reflected back to space, the atmosphere retains only 15%, and the earth's surface absorbs the remaining 43%. *Three times* as much energy is absorbed by the earth than is directly absorbed by the atmosphere, meaning the sun's rays don't heat the atmosphere directly. Instead the atmosphere is heated mostly from direct contact with the earth. The surface of the earth, being non-uniform, absorbs energy non-uniformly, ultimately heating the atmosphere non-uniformly. Dark fields, parking lots, rocks . . . these absorb more energy than do ponds, wet fields or forests. The warmer parts of the earth heat the atmosphere directly above them, which expands and lightens, eventually rising, much as can be seen in the steam from a teakettle's spout. As the heated air rises, cooler air flows in underneath it, is in turn heated and rises. This is a thermal. The rising air continues to expand as it goes up —

since there's less atmosphere above squeezing it together — while simultaneously cooling. If there is enough moisture in the air, a cloud may eventually form if the rising air mass cools to the 100% relative humidity point. In the United States, for all practical purposes, the bottom of the cloud marks the top of a thermal for sport glider pilots.

Even ridge lift is caused by the sun's heating. The air flowing into the bottom of thermals creates breezes. The larger the thermal, the larger its breezes. Combine a large enough breeze with a large enough obstacle, and ridge lift is the result. While the breezes of a size to create ridge lift are not caused by local thermals, the sun nevertheless is still the source of ridge lift breezes. A simple experiment illustrates how.

Hold a flashlight one foot above a sheet of paper and shine it vertically down; trace around the circle of light. Now, still one vertical foot away from the paper, hold the flashlight at a 45-degree angle and trace around the ellipse of light. The same amount of light energy hits the paper both times, but the first time it was concentrated, the second time more spread out. In essence, this is what happens to the earth. Solar energy hits the equatorial region with much more intensity than the polar regions. So warm air at the equator rises and is replaced by cooler air from the north and south. The warmed equatorial air rises, cools and moves poleward, high above the earth. As it sinks, it replaces the surface air which has moved toward the equator to take the place of the rising warmed air. All of the weather we experience results from this general global heating and subsequent air motion. In principle, it's elegantly simple; but, from the glider pilot's perspective, there are enough small-scale influences to make soaring an unending challenge and joy.

Rotation of the earth complicates the air motion, just described, by lending a twisting motion. For simplicity's sake, let's consider only the northern hemisphere, noting that each effect in the north has its near counterpart in the southern hemisphere, but the directions of rotation are reversed.

The rising air at the equator cannot rise forever, thanks to gravity. As it cools from expansion, it eventually begins to sink. Unable to go directly down because of the air swelling up beneath it, it begins to flow north, high above the earth's surface. The rotation of the earth — at the equator the surface of the earth is going approximately 1,000 m.p.h. to the east — causes the direction of this northerly flowing air to slowly bend toward its right, toward the east. By the time it has traveled roughly one third of the way from the equator to the north pole, it is moving directly eastward, still high above the earth. Here, it tends to pile up forming an area of higher pressure, and some — but not all — sinks back down to the surface.

Unable to penetrate into the earth, some of the sinking air is forced south and some is deflected north. The southerly flowing air is deflected to its right again, becoming the northeast tradewinds, which form the return flow into the equator. The northerly flowing air, again deflected to its right by the earth's rotation, becomes the *westerlies*, which dominate the middle latitudes' weather pattern, between 30 degrees and 60 degrees north. These largely influence the U.S.' weather. Meanwhile, the highest remainder of the sinking air originally elevated from the equator manages to continue its way north. As it travels it continues cooling, eventually sinking in the vicinity of the north pole, little resisted by the cold surface air there. Another high-pressure area builds at the pole as the sinking air is eventually forced south by the earth's surface. Turning to its right again, this air becomes the *polar easterlies*. Flowing from the northeast toward the southwest, this relatively cold air eventually contacts the westerlies around 60 degrees north latitude. This line of collision is called the *polar front* and is the source of much of the changing winter weather in the United States. The polar front tends to be farther north in summer than in winter, but at all times of the year the heavier, cold, polar-air mass tends to push beneath the warmer westerlies, causing outbreaks of cold weather as far south as Florida and Mexico.

The large-scale winds associated with the tradewinds, the polar front, and the westerlies are the breezes used by soaring pilots along the ridges.

In the 1930s, with the discovery of thermals, ridge soaring quickly came to be perceived as restrictive and limiting to cross-country soaring. Thirty years later in the United States, Karl Striedieck, a soaring pilot who was also a National Guard pilot flying from the Pittsburgh area, had the opportunity to gaze down on the Allegheny Mountain ridges from his F-106 at 40,000 feet. Contemplating the hundreds of miles of startlingly uniform ridges, and knowing of the strong north-westerly winds associated with polar-air-mass frontal passages, he began to wonder if those ridges and the frontal winds might be used to make world-record distance soaring flights. He did more than dream, though. He bought himself a used, German-built Schleicher K-8 glider, of modest performance for the day, launched himself in March of 1968 from the top of a ridge in central Pennsylvania, dove over its western edge and headed southwest. By day's end, Karl had flown 238 miles down the ridge, turned around and flown back to his starting point, for a total of 476 miles — a new world out and return record! A little over three years later, having lost his record to two more thermal-based flights, in November of 1971 Karl regained it with a flight of 569 miles. In October of the following year, he raised it twice more, to 682 miles.

By 1983, the record was up to 1023 miles! Although Karl was the first to fly more than 1,000 miles in a glider and has flown over 1000 miles at least twice along the ridges, he doesn't currently own the record, but he showed the way. Soaring is a sport the limitations of which are an intriguing mix of those self-imposed and those naturally imposed.

In 1937, a new type of lift was discovered in addition to ridge and thermal. Four years earlier in Silesia, located between Poland and Czechoslovakia, a soaring pilot was ridge soaring above the small town of Grunau, not far from the soaring school run by Wolf Hirth in Hirschberg. Flying as though in ridge lift, he found himself rising well above the ridge, much too high to still be in ridge lift, though he continued to use the technique required for ridge flying. That is, instead of circling as required by thermals, he merely held an angle sufficiently into the prevailing wind so as to not be blown back downwind.

As he tacked back and forth, first with the ridge to his back then with nothing but a growing expanse of sky behind him, Wolf Hirth (already a world-famous soaring pilot), watching from the airfield at Hirschberg, could contain his curiosity no longer. What was it that allowed the distant glider he could see climb to thermal heights while being flown in ridge soaring fashion? Clambering into the school's powerplane, he soon joined the glider and its equally puzzled, but elated pilot. The two of them continued to rise thousands of feet above the ridge, to thermal heights, the whole while flying back and forth parallel to the ridge now far below them, never circling. Strangest of all, though, the lift was glassily — even eerily — smooth, lacking the normal turbulence of ridge and thermal lift. This was something new!

By 1937, word of the phenomenon had spread throughout Germany, and other sailplane pilots had soon sampled this new form of lift, which always seemed to be located downwind of specific mountains. But that was all they knew. They didn't know how high it extended, or even what caused it. Until these questions could be answered, risks couldn't be assessed, nor could systematic learning take place; finding and utilizing this wonderfully strange new lift continued to be largely a matter of luck. In May of 1937, all of that changed at a glider contest held at Grunau.

The contest's organizers included Joachim Kuettner, who was working toward his second doctorate and who later became an internationally recognized expert in meteorological science; he also continued to hold a lifelong love for soaring. Displaying the organizational and intellectual acumen which would mark his subsequent career, he was instrumental in adding the requirement that all of this contest's flights were to carry barographs, and, in calling distance tasks in directions intended to allow the determination of the nature of this new lift. By subsequently plotting the areas of lift and sink shown on the barograph traces against the location of the glider at the times the traces were obtained, they quickly determined the new lift could only be a mountain wave.

Not long afterward, wearing a light shirt and shorts and without supplemental oxygen, Dr. Kuettner soared an open cockpit sailplane, from the Hirschberg site in the wave. He set an unofficial new world altitude record of 23,000 feet. On this flight, he was one of the first people to experience the symptoms of oxygen starvation — and survive. His original intention in making the flight was simply to learn something of the extent of the wave, not to risk his life, and the flight illustrates some of the hidden risks all pioneers face. In Kuettner's case, the plane's altimeter, reflecting the general needs of the time, indicated only up to 10,000 feet, which, once exceeded, meant he had no real idea of his altitude. Also, oxygen starvation is insidious. It sounds awful; images spring to mind of pilots with eyes bugged out, purpled faces, choking for breath. But all of these things are a result of stopping the breathing reflex, not of oxygen starvation; the reality is far different. So long as the breathing reflex isn't interfered with, you breathe normally as you climb. At 18,000 feet, you're above half of the available oxygen in the atmosphere. If you have ever exerted yourself at higher elevations, you'll have noted being easily winded. Sitting quietly in a sailplane cockpit, though, requires no more physical energy than sitting and reading this book; there is no exertion. All that happens, as you climb, is that, with each breath, you inhale less and less oxygen. What, then, are the effects? Sometimes . . . nothing! Eventually, you will just go to sleep. More insidiously, some people actually feel *better* as they climb and breathe less oxygen; they feel exhilarated, more attuned to their senses. They feel wonderful. They feel *great!* Eventually, they, too, happily pass out. It is, in fact, possible to feel *so* good from oxygen starvation that you recognize something is wrong — the more knowledgeable may even recognize *what* is wrong — but you feel too good to want to do anything about it! You've passed beyond the time of useful consciousness.

Go high enough and you'll die from lack of oxygen; but, the experience will prove very pleasant. In 1937, the knowledge about oxygen starvation we take for granted today wasn't widely known. Dr. Kuettner had been lucky.

As he rose ever higher in his humble, open cockpit sailplane, he got colder and colder. Huddled behind the minuscule windscreen, drawing in less and less oxygen with each breath, the young Joachim Kuettner gradually became disoriented and began to sense the world around him as a series of vaguely connected still lifes. When the cloud we now call a lenticular cloud, which had been above and behind him for much of the climb, suddenly appeared in front of the plane, he sensed something was seriously wrong. He determined to descend. He pulled on the spoiler handle. Nothing! The spoilers were frozen shut. The plane continued to climb relentlessly. His only option was to soar — in strong lift — for miles along the face of the cloud until he could fly around its end and allow himself to drift back into the wave's down side. Along the way, the plane began to violently vibrate, and he prepared to bail out. When he took his hands from the controls, the vibrations stopped. He attempted to fly again, and the plane instantly began to vibrate more and more violently. Again, he prepared to bail out and, again, the vibrations stopped. Finally, he dully recognized *he* was the source of the vibrations. He was shivering so fiercely from the cold that the motions transferred through his quivering arms and hands to the control stick, along the cables at the base of the stick to the controls, and finally back into the plane in response to the chattering controls!

Eventually, he descended below 10,000 feet where his brain and the altimeter again began to function. He was lost. He was still lost by the time it was necessary to land. Once on the ground, he learned he was in Poland, well to the southeast of Grunau. Ultimately, he contacted his friends back at Hirschberg, and a retrieve was effected. From the barograph trace, they learned he had exceeded the existing world altitude record by nearly 9,000 feet!

But you won't find any record of this flight in the record books. In fact, not until after World War II was Kuettner's unofficial record exceeded. For, in that time of the rising Nazi tide, Joachim Kuettner was found to be "politically incorrect" by ancestry. He soon found his talents no longer welcomed in the German glider community, which by then had been taken over as much else with potential military implications had been, by one of the pervasive Nazi war machine organizations.

Having once more discovered a new form of lift, extreme curiosity about the phenomenon gripped the soaring community, but, with the coming of World War II, exploration of waves took a back seat to global events. The questions, though, remained. What about the nature of the mountain wave? What causes them? How high do they go? Where do they tend to form? How common are they?

After the conclusion of World War II, the first major scientific investigation into the nature of waves took place. In the early 1950s, the Sierra Wave Project (headed by Dr. Kuettner) strove to answer these questions. At its conclusion, one sailplane pilot had died from oxygen starvation when he unwittingly allowed himself to run out of oxygen at 31,000 feet. Another survived by parachute after being thrown from his glider when it was torn apart by forces making it weigh 16 times normal. He was temporarily blinded by negative G forces on his body estimated at 20 Gs. The world sailplane altitude record had been raised to 44,255 feet. And another glider pilot had soared a twin-engined, World War II fighter plane — a P-38 *Lightning* weighing more than 7 tons — from 13,000 feet to above 30,000 feet — with both engines stopped! Three times! Clearly, waves were powerful features of the atmosphere. At the conclusion of the Sierra Wave Project, the soaring community had available a body of knowledge to make wave flying acceptably safe for both power pilots and sailplane pilots. While the former consider waves something of a turbulence-causing nuisance in their faster-flying planes, the pilots of slower flying, more buoyant sailplanes find that waves hold a strong appeal.

At first, the attraction of soaring pilots to waves was simple: altitude. From the Sierra Wave Project, soaring pilots came to understand that atmospheric waves extend far higher than humans can live without a full pressure suit. For the average soaring pilot today, the wave is "merely" another wonderful feature of nature to experience. Just as duration for duration's sake faded in appeal to soaring pilots in the 1930s, so did the appeal of height for height's sake fade in appeal to a later generation of sailplane pilots. Pilots strive to remain clear of its life-threatening edges. Few sailplane pilots today want to climb higher than 40,000 feet.

Waves are studies in contrasts. Typically created in a manner similar to the familiar ripple which forms downstream of a rock in a brook, waves contain both distressing violence and ethereal smoothness. Beneath them, and sometimes at their highest limits, exists all the violent energy you might imagine when billions of tons of rushing air are deflected by a mountain obstruction. Cascading over the crest of the mountain, torrents of air are compressed in the valley behind, finally to spring thousands of feet into the sky in powerful oscillations. These oscillations can extend hundreds of miles downwind of the obstruction causing them. Trapped beneath the very peak of the wave, at the same height as the mountain obstruction, is a violently rotating horizontal column of air called the *rotor*. Often the only route into the wave is by flying directly through this rotor. But once above the rotor, the air magically ceases its disorganized mixing; adjacent molecules happily visit with their neighbors in leisure. The flow within a wave is the aerial equivalent of marching military columns; the flow within the rotor is like the random bustle of humanity found in a crowded mall. This organized flow of air within waves is the magic of *laminar flow*. You can see laminar flow in the smoke from a cigarette; leaving the cigarette, the flow streams up in a straight line — it is laminar. Then, suddenly, it swirls into a disorganized mass — it becomes turbulent flow. Most of the atmosphere is naturally turbulent; waves are a laminar exception. The rarity alone would be sufficient attraction for sailplane pilots, even without the allure of height, for to fly in the laminar portion of a wave is to ride on nature's magic carpet.

Experiencing the eerily smooth, sheer power of a wave, rather than using waves to gain absolute altitude for altitude's sake, is the wave's lure today. Perhaps in the future the immense height attainable in them might also be used to set new distance records by hopping from wave to wave, gliding in a downwind direction, parallel to the wind's flow. Ray Lynskey's 1,250 mile, New Zealand wave flight actually flew *perpendicular* to the wind flow, utilizing the primary waves set up by the New Zealand Alps. Regardless, privileged indeed are the pilots who view the world from the form-fitting interior of a sailplane cockpit at 30,000 feet. For just as the grandeur of viewing the Grand Canyon from its rim incomparably overwhelms the same scene on a post card, so does the view from a sailplane cockpit compare to that through an airliner window.

With the discovery of waves, the last of the "big three" types of lift had been found. With a new knowledge of the atmosphere available to them, throughout the 1930s, U.S. pilots (although few in number compared to their counterparts in Europe) rapidly gained soaring skills which soon were reflected in the flights they made. Five years after Ralph Barnaby's 15 minute flight of 1929, the U.S. distance record was 158 miles and the altitude record was 6,233 feet. By World War II, the U.S. records had increased to 290 miles and 17,264 feet, while the world records were 465 miles (held by a Russian) and 22,424 feet (held by a German and set more than a year *after* Joachim Kuettner's flight). The U.S. duration record was 21 hours 34 minutes, set in 1931, while the world duration record was 36 hours 35 minutes, set in 1933. Sensibly, once it was recognized there were ridges against which the wind rarely stopped blowing (making the duration record simply a matter of pilot endurance) it was soon dropped as an official record category, since it did nothing to foster continued development of piloting skills or soaring knowledge.

Prior to the war there existed sufficient numbers of U.S. pilots to justify national soaring contests on a more-or-less annual basis, despite the hardships of the Great Depression. These early competitions began as contests of duration, then rapidly evolved into tasks flyable only through judicious use of thermals. In 1939, Chester Decker (eventual winner of the contest with 1,149 total miles) declared a goal 233 miles distant from Elmira, New York, then successfully soared to it. Because of the difficulties of predicting how the weather will develop in one single direction, hours in the future, soaring to a goal is *much* more difficult than simply following the best weather as it develops. The difficulty is reflected in the shorter distance required for today's Diamond Goal flight versus Diamond Distance.

In the U.S., after World War II's conclusion, the sport of soaring underwent a gradual but significant transition from a localized activity, existing primarily in the form of college clubs in the east and individuals in the west, to an activity which today is enjoyed in every state by thousands of people. The notable exceptions prior to the war to the essentially local clubs and individuals were Elmira, New York, and Torrey Pines, California, the two locations which came closest to being identified as "national" sites. After the war, the nature of the clubs changed from primarily college-affiliated, to groups of private individuals banding together to share costs of soaring. Recently, while not nearly so prevalent as before the war, college clubs are once again becoming more common. In the postwar prosperity, commercial soaring operations came into being. Today, commercial operations often exist symbiotically on fields which also contain club operations. They can be found in most states, usually near larger population centers.

The emphasis on record flights decreased somewhat after the war as it became more difficult to set new ones, and as a consequence more emphasis was placed on recognizing individual achievement in the form of various badges awarded through the Soaring Society of America. From the 1940s through the 1980s, most soaring pilots stalked the internationally recognized Silver, Gold and Diamond Badges. The Silver Badge is intended to develop the self-reliance of the new soaring pilot. The Gold Badge encourages pilots to more fully develop the skills gained in pursuit of the Silver Badge. The Diamond Badge is designed to extend pilots to their limits. For all practical purposes, Diamond Altitude gain requires flight in a wave.

As the performance of sailplanes continues to improve in parallel with growing overall piloting skills, additional recognition of longer flights has become necessary. Today there is a 1,000-kilometer diploma, and a host of speed records are kept, as well, down to the state level. So far, most — but not all — of the 1,000-kilometer (621.4-mile) flights in the U.S. are made along the Allegheny ridges. Further exploration of soaring possibilities could change this. The very first 1,000-kilometer flight in the world was flown in 1964 from Odessa, Texas, to Kimball, Nebraska, by Alvin Parker in thermals, several years before Karl Striedieck "discovered" the ridges. Parker used an American-designed and built *Sisu* sailplane.

Today, the sport of soaring offers joy and challenges to meet all manner of interests, ranging from commercial rides (in two seaters flown by licensed pilots) given as presents, to local fun flights, to badge flying, to lengthy for-fun-only cross-country flights, to contest flying, to record flying. The participant can stretch his or her skills as far — or as little — as they are comfortable. For the non-pilot, the rewards range from the thrill of a new experience, to escape into a previously but dimly imagined world. For the soaring pilot, the rewards are equally varied. Pilots who have flown hundreds of miles on better days can be equally challenged on lesser days simply to remain aloft. The rewards are measured, not simply in miles or miles per hour or feet, but in more esoteric commodities: the confidence gained from controlling a vehicle in three dimensions; the unforgettable thrill of your first solo and your first climb as pilot in command; the pleasure of taking a child, a friend, a loved one, for a sailplane ride; soaring with Red Tail Hawks in the gentle smoothness of late evening thermals when the world below is bathed in warm, golden light; making the perfect landing. To slip the bonds of earth is to change yourself forever into a three-dimensional creature who will never again view the world as before. To soar is to join the realm of the birds and gradually gain the knowledge that the world belongs to its creatures in a way that transcends geographic and political boundaries. And we are privileged to gain this insight, not from the rigors of a political or religious discussion, but in the cathedral of the sky bounded only by nature and our own personal visions.

Chapter Eight

The Planes

After soaring now for over two decades, the author has not had one single person walk up and ask, "How come your glider is so ugly?" On the other hand, he has had un-counted strangers rush up, wide-eyed in excitement, to exclaim they'd never seen anything so beautiful in their entire lives as his sailplane. At times like these he envies the people who have designed and built these planes, for there is not much man creates which instantly destroys the barriers between total strangers in such a positive manner. His experience in this regard is not unusual in any way, nor is there is anything unique about any of the sailplanes he's owned over the years. By owning a sailplane — *any* sailplane — he has become simply another witness to the profound influence on human emotions exerted by them. Sailplanes are an ultimate expression of form following function. Artwork intended for flight, they are truly beautiful. Timeless words like *sleek, graceful* and *elegant* spice the conversation of many; in the vernacular, *cool, far out* and *awesome* rate equal time. Whatever the words, they're but an expression of something more deeply felt by those viewing sailplanes up close who have not yet become inured to their presence. No one will ever mistake a sail-plane for anything else than a creation designed to slip silently through the air while gliding great distances.

The very first time the author beheld a sailplane was from the small forward opening of its trailer. His eyes had not yet adjusted to the darkness of the below-grade garage. The sailplane was illuminated only from light flaring in from the open garage door, precious little of which seeped around his torso into the interior of the trailer as he strained to see within its confines. Nestled dimly within, lit only by the few lumens reflected from the bottoms of the wings framing it, was a sleek, circular fuselage, topped by a canopy darkly glistening. The canopy sloped impossibly away from him, swallowed in the black recesses of the trailer. There was a heart-stopping perfection in the shining surfaces, unmarred by any break, any flaw, any insult to the curved reflections. He was struck dumb by this vision of unspeakable beauty. The type of ship he was viewing, an AS-W 12 manufactured by the German firm of Alexander Schleicher Flugzeugbau, meant nothing to him; all that mattered was the ship itself. The following weekend saw the vision assembled for flight at the airport, its beauty undiminished in the unsparing light of day.

Wings spanning 60 feet slid into fittings mounted high on the fuselage. Forward of the wings projected a cockpit designed for a single, supine pilot. There was no wasted space within. Beneath the clear plexiglass, exposing fully the top half of the circular fuselage ahead of the wings, could be seen starkly functional rudder pedals for the pilot's feet, not 6 inches from the nose; six feet farther aft a headrest graced the rear of the cockpit. Perched on the fuselage centerline immediately forward of the control stick was a small, black pedestal containing less than half a dozen instruments and meant obviously to be straddled by the pilot's legs on their journey to the rudder pedals. On both cockpit walls, various control levers sprouted where the pilot's hands would be once he lay within. The entire cockpit was less than 24 inches wide. Extending aft, seemingly forever, was an impossibly slim, round tailboom. Protruding skyward from the very tip of the tailboom was a vertical stabilizer ending at eye height. Mounted atop, like some fantastic razor blade, was a thin horizontal stabilizer.

This gleaming white chariot of the skies was supported by a stalky landing gear which lent the ship an air of aloof anticipation as it rested slightly askew, one wingtip braced against the earth it seemed so eager to leave behind. Gear doors sticking down gave mute evidence this excrescence was merely a necessary evil required for takeoff and landing; it was obviously intolerable during flight.

By the time the author saw the "12" assembled, he'd learned its compound curves and gleaming white exterior masked a structure of high-strength fiberglass; the "12" itself was one of the first gliders of composite construction to enter production, and, as it sat resplendent on the ramp, it represented a revolution in the design and performance of gliders. It presaged a time when high performance would become available to the average pilot, and the "12" was the temporary pinnacle. Such emphasis had been placed during its design on maximizing glide performance that no cutouts for spoilers marred its wing surfaces; the only way this sleek white craft had of creating the drag so necessary for landing was to release a parachute from beneath the vertical stabilizer! Without the 'chute extended, the "12" could glide 47 feet forward for every foot down, the first glider to simply *ignore* the 40:1 "barrier". Today, nearly three decades after it was designed and built, the "12" remains in the supership class. Its quest for high performance contained its Achilles' heel, though, for the 'chute design was of questionable reliability, resulting in inevitable landing accidents among the ships imported into the country. The owner of the one which so awed the author had designed, engineered and was troubleshooting a second 'chute housed within the wheelwell. It could be deployed in series or in parallel with the factory 'chute, acting either as a backup should the factory's malfunction, or as additional drag. Presuming both parachutes functioned as intended, this particular "12" could be shoehorned into fields smaller than the trainer, in which the author soon began taking lessons, could safely fit. Watching it descend was breathtaking.

The AS-W 12 proved to be a harbinger of composite sailplane design with its high wing and T-tail. To the uninitiated, composite sailplanes are much more similar in appearance than all-metal, steel-tube-and-fabric, or wood-and-fabric sailplanes. Regardless of the structural material, though, there's no mistaking a sailplane for anything else. If you removed the engine from a powerplane, faired in the engine compartment and added the weight needed to compensate for removal of the engine, you would have — a powerplane with its engine removed. In strong wave lift, it would even be capable of soaring. But it would never be mistaken for a sailplane. The essence of sailplanes is the distinctive nose extended forward, using the pilot's weight to balance the craft longitudinally, and the endless wings.

How Come?

The price of movement through the atmosphere is *drag*. The price of supporting planes' weight is a form of drag induced by the wings themselves passing through the air as they create lift. Out at the wingtips, air leaks from the side with higher pressure to the side with lower pressure, creating a swirling motion. All wings generate these *tip vortices*; sometimes you can see them in head-on videotapes of jet aircraft landing or taking off. And when a wing has to work harder to support the weight of the plane, as it must do at slow speeds, these vortices are their strongest. At low speeds, this lift-induced, vortex drag becomes an increasing percentage of the airplane's total drag, until, at the low speeds necessary for thermalling flight, it has become a significant portion of the sailplane's total drag. Practical experience, wind tunnel tests and mathematical theories indicate long, narrow wings can measurably reduce the amount of induced drag created by a wing. Hence, true sailplanes have such wings.

Distinctive noses and long wings have been present in sailplanes since the mid 1920s. In the early development of new, man-carrying machines, designers tried all manner of configurations, searching for the best compromise between comfort and control for the owner, cost of manufacturing, practicability and other considerations. This experimentation was notably true with airplanes and automobiles. In the first 20 years of each one's existence, if a configuration could be imagined and built, it was. But, in time, the best configuration comes to predominate. In the case of sailplanes, in which form is inseparable from function, as early as 1930, sailplanes became unquestionably sailplanes and nothing else. Yet, examine these creations in detail, and significant differences between designs down the years emerge.

Throughout the 1920s and 1930s, the higher-performance sailplanes of the day were almost exclusively built from wood. It was plentiful, many people had practical experience with it, a body of engineering data existed for it and — terribly important for sailplanes — it was simultaneously light, strong and capable of being shaped into smooth, wind-cheating curves. Initially, so long as soaring flight was confined to the ridges, the importance of minimizing lift-induced drag was largely ignored by designers, and long wings were actually something of a nuisance. But when thermalling flight became the norm in the early 1930s, of necessity wingspans grew rapidly. The *Moatzagotl,* designed in the early 1930s, had a span exceeding 60 feet; the *Austria* spanned 90 feet! Eventually, a practical limit of wood-span wings of around 55 to 60 feet was reached. Beyond that, soarability suffered due to excessive weight and slow control response. Weight is primarily a rigging limitation; a single-piece wing is heavy, while multiple-piece wings become an assembly nuisance. Adequate control response remains something of a limiting factor today, although the maximum spans available on today's highest-performance production ships stretches once again to exceed 80 feet! Much more common, though, are gliders with spans of 50 feet.

Early gliders utilized skids, rather than wheels, for landing gears. So long as most flying was done from grass fields, as was the case throughout the 1930s, skids were excellent. Gradually, though, the practicability of wheels came to predominate, and, today, a glider with a skid is viewed by most as something of an anachronism, although almost all Schweizer designs utilize a helper-skid forward of the main wheel. A wheel/skid design is a good compromise for ground-handling reasons, if perhaps draggy and somewhat labor intensive on hard surfaces, since the skid plate must be replaced regularly.

Enclosed sailplane cockpits came into common use immediately after World War II due, as most advances in sailplane design are, to the demands of increased performance. Prior to that time, open-cockpit drag reduction had come in the form of more and more sophisticated cockpit fairings replacing — initially — nothing. Eventually, simple wind deflectors were designed merely to decrease pilot discomfort. Ultimately, the unceasing search for ever-increased performance led, inevitably, first to enclosed canopies and then to retractable landing gears. At low speeds, the drag of a wheel protruding into the airstream, even a well-faired one, is a small percentage of the total drag of the sailplane. But, at higher speeds, wheel drag becomes significant. In the quest for ever greater inter-thermal speeds, fixed wheels had to go.

In their quest for performance, designers also sought inspiration from nature, particularly the graceful wheeling flight of seagulls. Some of the most graceful sailplanes ever built were the superships of the 1930s. Imitation of nature extended even to "gull wings" in sailplanes: wings with a pronounced upward slant at the fuselage, the dihedral extending to mid-span where the wings crooked back to horizontal. Seen from below, these wing tips swept gently and gracefully aft, much like a bird's. Completing the avian illusion was the lacquered, cotton fabric which covered much of the wings, and through which the sun shone in magnificent translucence. Wheeling majestically in overhead thermals, you see silhouetted against the sky wing spars and shape-giving wing ribs, the sailplane-bird's skeleton. In the presence of these wood-and-fabric creations, it's impossible not to feel a kinship with the forces of nature, even while doing no more than watching from below.

Not every glider can be a world-beater, and more and more intermediate performance ships came to be manufactured with welded, steel-tube fuselages covered by fabric. This construction was both less costly and more rugged than the hollow-wood shells of higher-performance sailplanes. Wings of these intermediate ships were either of the familiar wood-and-fabric construction, or aluminum-and-fabric construction, and they were often strut braced instead of cantilevered directly from the fuselage. Use of aluminum provided cost savings, because wing ribs could be formed in a single piece rather than from many individual pieces. Struts were deemed an acceptable compromise for ships intended for local use rather than long flights; they helped in part to reduce the weight of these ships, making them somewhat easier for the intermediate pilot to thermal than a higher performance plane.

With the advent of routine thermalling flights, designers initially concentrated on minimizing the thermalling sink rate of the new sailplanes. Consequently, ships of the middle and late 1930s through the mid 1950s tended to be "floaters." Maximizing the rate of climb in thermals was the primary design goal, because it was the height gained in thermals which made longer soaring flights possible. In the arena of the sky, though, nothing comes without a price, and the price paid by floaters was difficulty making progress over the ground in the face of a headwind. Consequently, most long flights during this period were made in a downwind direction or on days with light winds. Too often, the pilot of a floater found himself thermalling over the same field more than once as he tried to penetrate into the wind. Flying upwind was like flying through molasses. Each time he stopped to circle in a thermal, he found himself drifting in the wind field with the thermal, going the opposite direction from his desires. Upon leaving the thermal, if the wind was blowing 20 m.p.h. aloft, he would have to fly faster than normal in order to make acceptable headway, but, the faster he flew, the more rapid his descent. Floaters eventually proved too specialized for most pilots, who sought the ability to soar in any direction of their choosing on the good soaring days.

One means of minimizing a floater's handicap was to carry ballast in the glider. By intentionally making the glider weigh more, the pilot knowingly sacrificed some climb performance in exchange for a flatter glide at higher speeds. In order to support the increased weight, the glider simply must fly faster when comparing speeds at some arbitrary glide angle. Early forms of weight were shot bags or lead bars placed in or just behind the cockpit. One drawback was the impossibility of jettisoning these weights if the plane flew into weaker conditions on course, where the ballast became a liability. Some form of disposable ballast was obviously preferable, but nothing practicable could be devised. Nevertheless, for years, pilots bent on maximizing their speed, or minimizing the effects of headwinds on strong soaring days, carried forms of non-disposable ballast.

In the 1950s, sailplane designers began trying to gain the benefits of ballast without paying its penalties. They used flaps positioned at the trailing edge of the wings, inboard of the ailerons. By bending the trailing edge of the wing down slightly at the flap joint when thermalling, a wing could generate more lift. This meant that a glider could be heavier, allowing improved high speed flight, while still being able to effectively utilize weak thermals. Flaps came into common use about the same time another design innovation occurred — all-aluminum gliders. As inter-thermal flight speeds increased, it became more important to maintain smooth flow over wings and fuselage in order to reduce high-speed turbulence and drag. This was particularly difficult to do with wooden structures, which tend to naturally have surface ripples, in addition to being prone to shrink and swell with changes in humidity. With age, wood ships also generally tend to take on a starved look as the wood covering shrinks slightly around the reinforcing internal wing ribs and fuselage frames. While not reducing strength or adversely affecting flying characteristics in an obvious way, these protrusions all serve to generate turbulent — and draggy — flow in the layer of air adjacent the glider's skin, reducing its performance from what it would be if the surfaces were smooth.

All-aluminum ships addressed this surface smoothness problem and simultaneously provided a strong, weather-resistant exterior. Although aluminum resulted in a heavier structure than wood, flaps and a generation of pilots primed for the benefits of heavier ships combined to mitigate the adverse effects of weight. So long as a glider isn't so heavy that attaching its wings is a major chore, the basic problem with weight is one of speed. Like all airplanes, a sailplane's only means of support is the lift generated by its wings. All wings generate lift by the reaction principle. By deflecting air downward, wings generate an upward reacting force; they generate lift. To support the weight of a sailplane and its pilot, the wing must deflect downward hundreds of pounds of air. In a steady glide, where the speed isn't changing, you can imagine the slower a glider flies the harder the wing must work to throw air down, because there's less air, per second, for the wing to work with, compared to a glide at a higher speed. The only way the wing can throw more air per second downward is by angling its leading edge more steeply upward into the wind. The slower the glider flies, the steeper this angle must be or the glider does what anything does if its weight isn't supported. It falls! Go slowly enough and, eventually, such a steep angle is reached that the air no longer flows smoothly around the wing, but separates; the wing "stalls", and the glider falls until it regains flying speed.

It's this *stalling angle* that determines thermalling speeds. The slower a sailplane can fly, the smaller its turning radius. Since thermals tend to be strongest at their centers, the smaller its turning radius, the better the sailplane's potential climb rate. Since the cross-sectional shapes (*airfoils*) used for glider wings all tend to stall at about the same *angle of attack*, a heavier sailplane translates directly into higher stalling speeds. This, in turn, requires higher thermalling speeds, which means the plane circles in weaker lift. Thus, the climb rate problem isn't weight itself, it's the *speed* necessitated by the weight.

Flaps offer something of a panacea. By bending the aft portion of a wing down slightly, the original airfoil is changed, and the new airfoil is capable of generating more lift at a given speed than the unbent airfoil can. *Voila!* Slower thermalling speeds return. The extra drag associated with the bent airfoil is more than compensated for by the ability to remain in the strongest portion of the thermals.

Flaps are the closest thing to magic in the sailplane designer's bag of tricks. Prior to their introduction, it was typical for each square foot of glider wing to have to support 3 to 5 pounds in flight. With the advent of flaps, the amount of weight supported by each square foot of wing — the *wing loading* — increased by about 2 pounds to 5-7 pounds per square foot.

Never content with a good thing, all-aluminum wings also opened up a completely new ballast avenue for pilots to explore because, even though the newer ships weren't floaters, the same reasoning applied to making even them heavier. Water came into use as ballast. Universally available, dense and most importantly — disposable — water makes a near ideal ballast. Its two drawbacks are that it freezes and it's wet! Early attempts to confine it within the open space inside metal wings employed sealed, vinyl bags, which often leaked. While sometimes physically unpleasant (when it leaked into the cockpit) and always something of a concern (due to weight shifts in a metal ship when it leaked), it was no longer the rot, weakened wood and glue hazard which prevented its use in wooden ships. Today, capability for carrying water ballast is standard on sailplanes.

But higher wing loadings and water ballast were not the reasons all-aluminum ships were created, lower drag was. In this, expectations were also met. Metal ships could be designed and built which had extensive areas of smooth, laminar flow over fuselage and wing surfaces. Glide ratios improved dramatically, particularly at higher speeds.

A high performance ship of the mid 1930s had a maximum glide ratio of around 30:1 and would sink six feet every second at a speed of 66 m.p.h. The glide ratio at 66 m.p.h. was only 16:1. (The speed equating to a six-feet-per-second sink rate is typically used as a convenient estimation of a glider's higher-speed performance.) The very best of the wooden ships never had a maximum glide ratio much above 36:1, and a six-feet-per-second sink speed of perhaps 80 m.p.h. At 80 mph and six-fps sink, the glide ratio isn't quite 20:1.

A typical, flapped, metal ship of the generation before composites came into general use had a maximum glide ratio of close to 40:1, a six-fps sink speed of 90 mph and a 6 fps glide ratio of 22:1. Most of the metal ships' performance increases occurred at high speeds, a result of smooth surfaces and laminar flow.

The use of all-aluminum structures in sailplanes proved a major advance. Yet its use was overshadowed in barely a decade when another material, promising even smoother surfaces and more extensive laminar flow, came into use. *Composites* burst upon the soaring scene. Today we lump an amazing collection of materials under the "composite" umbrella, and hardly a production sailplane is made that doesn't employ a carefully concocted mix of resin, fiberglass, carbon and aramid (e.g. Kevlar®) fiber to both shape it and carry loads. The first successful composite sailplane flew in 1957, in Germany. By the mid 1960s, a steadily increasing trickle promised to become a flood of composite imports into the U.S., as pilots fell in love with their looks as much as with their ease of assembly and care and uniformly high performance. Being a plastic material prior to cure of the resin, volume production of sailplanes with smooth surfaces and compound curves became commonplace; the uncured material could be laid up in female molds of any shape possible to machine. Even better, the material retains its shape well as it ages, and it has an unknown — possibly unlimited — life span if not exposed to physical abuse. Oddly, the first generation of composite sailplanes, which exclusively employed glass fibers, were still heavier than metal ships, but their smooth contours made for better overall performance, and, once in use, there was no looking back.

In the 1970s, the introduction of carbon fibers tended to lighten the composite ships somewhat, but a person cannot tell from its appearance what kind of fibers a composite sailplane contains. A person *can* be fairly certain if the ship they are looking at is composite, though. Nearly all of them are unremittingly white, to keep them cool in the sun, since the resins tend to lose some of their strength if warmed, even though fully cured. Better safe then sorry applies to their color schemes.

Twenty years before the military, commercial airliner manufacturers, lightplane manufacturers, or anyone else in the airplane manufacturing business, saw fit to use composites for primary aircraft structure, glider manufacturers were routinely doing so, with an excellent safety record.

Composite sailplanes burst on the American soaring world with startling suddenness and lasting impact. Pilots who were previously perfectly satisfied with their wood or metal ships suddenly felt impelled to sell them to finance their new, composite purchase. Almost overnight, wooden planes passed from the hands of active pilots to those more interested in flying them as museum and historical pieces. Metal planes took on a second-class status, despite often very little performance differences between them and a newer composite ship. But not a pilot breathes who doesn't dream of flying the very best, and the very best of the composite ships today have performance so outstandingly good that most non-glider pilots have difficulty imagining what it would be like to fly one.

Consider the AS-W 12, which so profoundly touched the author's inner sense of beauty more than 20 years ago (and today remains one of the most beautiful of sailplanes to him). It has a maximum glide ratio of 47:1 and a speed at six-fps sink of over 100 mph. The *best* of today's ships have glide angles so flat and glide ratios so high — perhaps 60:1 — that measuring their performance is quite difficult. The speed at six-fps sink approaches 110 mph, for a glide ratio of nearly 27:1. (To put that in perspective, the composite ship in which the author has happily flown thousands of miles since 1981 has a *maximum* glide ratio little better than 35:1.) Such a supership, starting from less than 5,000 feet above the ground at Washington, D.C., could glide beyond Baltimore before having to enter a landing pattern. Starting from less than 10,000 feet — a good day, but not an impossibility in the east — it could glide from Philadelphia to New York City without having to climb. On an average western day it could easily glide the 124 miles from Los Angeles to San Diego without circling.

As the AS-W 12 made use of a parachute to help it descend for landing, so must every other sailplane, manufactured since World War II, have some method of adding drag or spoiling lift in order to land. All manner of devices are used. Look beyond the eye-catching acres of white wing surfaces down to the faint seams, marking the edges of control surfaces. You'll see the outlines of the numerous kinds of landing devices: top-only spoilers, top and bottom spoilers, two-piece spoilers, spoilers so big they're actually dive brakes capable of letting the truly brave pilot point the plane straight at the ground and still keep him below redline, 90° flaps, flaps with leading edges which protrude into the airflow atop the wing, rotating plates and more.

And while you're at it, check the bottom of the vertical stabilizer for the seam that indicates a parachute lurks within. While only the "12" was so bold to entirely dispense with spoilers or anything beyond a one-shot parachute, other gliders have used parachutes as auxiliary landing aids.

Each device has its advantages and disadvantages, its supporters and detractors. All of the devices work by adding drag, while some also add lift, permitting slower touchdown speeds. Should they fail to work (usually because you have failed to connect them properly), as a last resort, you can attempt to land from a *slip*. By flying the sailplane sideways to the air, you can use the drag of the fuselage to increase the sailplane's descent rate. With older ships, slips were an effective and common means of regulating the ship's descent rate in the landing pattern. With the slim fuselages of composite ships, slips lose much of their effectiveness: the plane flies sideways, startling the casual observer, but doesn't come down rapidly *while* flying sideways, startling the pilot. Probably, most pilots of composite ships would find it impossible to safely land their steeds on anything but an international airport, without resort to the sailplane's normal landing aids.

How Well Does It Work?

Sailplanes achieve their flattest glide angle at low speeds, yet, in order to fly long distances high speeds are necessary. How fast can sailplanes fly? *Redlines* — the speed above which the designer says you're playing Test Pilot — on most composite sailplanes are in the 165-mph range. Redline on the low-performance, single seater many people first transition to is 103 mph. A better measure than redline, though, is the speeds gliders achieve when the need to replenish their altitude is factored in. What average speed can they achieve over a course, from the time they cross a starting line in the air to the time they cross an aerial finish line? In 1983, at Hobbs, New Mexico, in the World Gliding Championships, 12 pilots of the 19 flying a 324-mile triangle *averaged* over 100 mph. The fastest pilot that day averaged 110 mph! To show it wasn't a fluke, the very next contest day, on an even longer triangle of 354 miles, the winner averaged 106 mph and four pilots averaged over 100 mph. Admittedly, these pilots were all flying superships, but some pilots of ships in the 15-Meter Class — the type of ship commonly found at any gliderport (whose only design restriction is a 15 meter — 49.2 feet — limit on wing span) — also averaged over 100 mph on two days! On a 254-mile triangle, the winner averaged 102 mph, and on another 296-mile triangle, the winner averaged nearly 101 mph. All of these flights used thermals; Hobbs has no ridges.

On the Allegheny ridges, where it's not necessary to stop and thermal on days when the winds blow steadily from the northwest, average speeds are even higher; the fastest flight known to the author averaged 125 mph over a distance of nearly 190 miles!

More typical speeds achieved by the sport soaring pilot today range from 50-90 mph. Even on the strongest days, beginners in composite ships find themselves struggling to average more than 50 mph; only with experience and elimination of much unnecessary climbing do higher speeds come. Soon after obtaining his license, in a low-performance ship in which experienced pilots have averaged over 50 mph, on the author's very first successful cross-country flight, he averaged 12 mph! His average speed on a decent day in his 15-meter ship tends to be between 60 and 70 mph without water ballast, and he has approached 80 mph, occasionally, carrying ballast. The author can only imagine the unrelenting pounding experienced by pilots flying fast in the turbulence along the Allegheny ridges.

These, then, are the sailplanes themselves, the creations which make all soaring flight possible. From wooden floater to fiberglass supership, they permit the pilot to enter the realm of thousands of years of dreams, the realm formerly sole dominion of the birds.

Chapter Nine

People

Soaring attracts to it some truly remarkable people. Beyond those aerial aces — the aerial stars of the sport, winners of national and international competitions and pilots with world-record-setting soaring skills — beyond them lie a host of outwardly normal people who would no sooner toot their own horn than dance naked in the streets. From among this gathering of people is a considerable proportion who have quietly chosen to pour significant energies and enthusiasm into the sport, always benefiting it and sometimes providing major advances. As a sport utterly dependent upon using nature's forces efficiently, soaring often surrenders advances to the relentlessly logical and is peopled by a high percentage of engineers, many of whom succumb to the unsolved challenges of the sport. The more driven of these people dedicate considerable portions of their adult personal and business lives to solving these challenges.

Few among those who dream of and practice motorless flight can't easily fantasize of designing or creating or flying world-beating superships in international competition. Some do more than fantasize, as, for example, Gerhard Waibel, de-

signer of the AS-W 12 and, as of this writing, seven other sailplanes, all of which have been manufactured by the Alexander Schleicher firm. Waibel has been designing, building and test-flying sailplanes for a living since graduating college in the mid-1960s, and he continues to do so today. Four of his ships are currently in production, and various of his designs have won numerous World Championships.

Until his premature death in 1994, his college classmate, Klaus Holighaus, was chief designer of the Schempp-Hirth Company following his graduation. Somewhat more prolific as a designer than Waibel, Holighaus not only flew his designs in World and many National Championships, he won. More than once!

A third classmate, Wolf Lemke, went on to form his own sailplane manufacturing company, Lemke-Schneider. Like Waibel and Holighaus, he is still very much active as a designer, and he has also experienced the satisfaction of seeing several of his designs win World Championships through the years.

In the United States, three brothers from New York, Ernie, Bill and Paul Schweizer, built — in their father's hayloft — and flew their first sailplane in 1930. They went on to form the Schweizer Aircraft Corporation in 1939. With uncommon Yankee common sense they guided SAC through 45 years of sailplane production. So great was their interest in the sport that, until Bill Schweizer in 1991 wrote the book *Soaring With the Schweizers: The Fifty-Year History of Their Aviation Adventures,* few U.S. soaring pilots understood that the production of sailplanes was always a sideline for the company. Many thought sailplanes were the *only* products SAC built. (Only once did sales from sailplanes exceed 20% of SAC's total sales dollars in a year. Although SAC's last pure sailplane was manufactured in 1984, the company remains in the Schweizer family's hands, being run by a second generation of Schweizer pilots.)

More correctly, the Schweizers are generally credited with nurturing the sport in the U.S. after World War II, some would even say preserving it, for the better times to follow.

Rarely concentrating their energies on the design of super-high performance planes, the Schweizers built, instead, rugged, two-seat, training sailplanes and medium- to high-performance single seaters. They favored metal designs for crashworthiness reasons. Their only wooden sailplane was produced for the U.S. military during World War II, after aluminum was requisitioned for higher priority production. All the author's initial training and first 150 hours of soaring experience was achieved in two Schweizer designs, which continue to be used for primary instruction today. Though Schweizer sailplanes were rarely world beaters, they were always ruggedly built, docile to fly and easy to land. The Schweizers and their company built more than 2,100 sailplanes over the years.

In Ohio, from the mid 1950s through the 1980s, Dick Schreder designed and built a series of metal (and later metal and composite) sailplanes, all designed for individuals to build either from plans or kits. Known as "HP" sailplanes (for High Performance, naturally), Schreder placed third in the 1963 World Championships in his HP-11 and won the U.S. Nationals in his HP-14 in 1966. Two characteristics of nearly all the HP-series are V-tails and the use of landing flaps instead of spoilers. With its powerful flaps, the HP-14, despite its championship-winning performance, could approach more steeply and slowly to, and safely land in, smaller fields than any other sailplane in the world — a tremendous safety advantage.

The ship the author has been flying since 1981, the *Zuni*, is the brainchild of another remarkable person and designer, George Applebay. George's dream was to make an American, composite sailplane second to none in the world in performance. Initially, he designed and built an Open Class ship, the *Mescalero*. (All Applebay designs are named after Indian tribes native to New Mexico, where he lives.) Deciding his limited resources could be more effectively utilized trying to produce a less expensive, 15-Meter-Class sailplane, he designed the *Zuni*, and, in the course of production, approximately 20 were built. First pulled from the molds in 1976 and 1977, *Zunis* were never destined to win a National or World Championship, but their distinctive shape remains

competitive in the 15-Meter Class. Were the author to come in last in a 15-Meter contest, the fault would be his and not the airplane's. Today, George and his son run a composite sailplane Repair Station in New Mexico, and a person doesn't have to look hard to see low-key George's animation level rise a couple of notches in the presence of one of his creations.

While sailplanes are very visible, and unquestionably the hardware stars of the sport, other people than sailplane designers have contributed mightily to its continued development, often in relative obscurity. People like Wil Schuemann, the author's first post-college officemate, and the person who introduced him to the sport. When the author met Wil, he saw a man of slight bearing in his early thirties. Probably 5'8" or 5'9" in height, he appeared shorter and smaller than he was because of a characteristic of standing with both hands in his back pockets, slightly stooped at the shoulders when he was in thought, or simply speaking with friends. A narrow face above a square chin was topped by a set of serious, dark eyes beneath a high forehead made more prominent by hair combed straight back in a dry pompadour. Wil proved to be a quiet, thoughtful person, not given to speaking lightly when his opinion was sought. Wil was not only a frighteningly competent engineer, but directed considerable of his energies toward soaring. His goal was to support himself by inventing and directly marketing his products to end users. Although we shared an office for barely 11 months, soon after which Wil left to go into business for himself, simply by continuing to enjoy the sport, the author and thousands of others have been privileged to benefit from a number of his inventions.

Prior to their meeting, Wil had already owned a Schweizer 1-26 (a low- to medium-performance sport glider) and a Glasflugel *Libelle* (a 15-Meter ship and one of the first composite ships to enter the U.S. in quantity). The aluminum and fabric-covered wings of most Schweizer sailplanes are notorious for "oil-canning" in turbulence, and the little 1-26 was no exception. At the time, living in an apartment with a young family, Wil decided to see if the performance of the 1-26 could be improved by better maintaining the airfoil's shape, a task mechanically similar to performing body work on a car. One wing at a time they became wintertime living room objects while he filled and sanded, checking and rechecking wing contours. When satisfied with the wings, he then went to great lengths to seal the many gaps and openings from which pressurized fuselage air could leak out in aerodynamically undesirable places, thereby raising drag. Several years after the event, he laughingly admitted that 1-26 owners could stop worrying about sealing the fuselage or filling the irregularities in their wings in hopes of increasing its performance. It wouldn't make the slightest difference!

The New Sailplane That Wasn't

This time-eating experiment in engineering knowledge didn't faze Wil after he traded up to the *Libelle*. Understand that most people owning a *Libelle* at the time were so awestricken with its performance that the thought of doing anything to mar its factory finish brought terror to their hearts. And to suggest its performance wasn't good enough was proof of a person's insanity. To begin cutting holes in one, attempting to actually *improve* its performance, marked a person as dangerous.

Wanting to make the *Libelle* as good as newer, long-winged, Open-Class ships of the day, Wil set about improving the plane where he could. As delivered, the aft portion of the *Libelle's* canopy mated directly with the top surfaces of each wing root. Believing the slightly pressurized ventilation air inside the cockpit should not be allowed to escape near the wing roots where it could prematurely trip the smooth laminar flow into higher drag, turbulent flow, Wil sought a way to eliminate the possibility; he wanted the air to exit at the rudder. He did two things. First, he cut down the rear of the canopy to make it smaller, so he could enclose the open top of the fuselage by building a fiberglass and resin shell. Having never worked with plexiglass canopies, or fiberglass and resin prior to this, Wil faced a daunting learning curve. Canopies, in particular, are beasts to work on, being fragile and large enough to be hideously awkward. Breaking one would mean an expensive delay while a replacement was shipped from Germany. Second, he cut holes in the aft fuselage at the base of the rudder for exhaust air vents and crafted streamlined fiberglass fairings over them to keep drag to a minimum. Both of these modifications were done with such skill and old-world craftsmanship as to make the modifications virtually indistinguishable from factory work.

But Wil didn't stop there. He next completely revised the factory airfoil. Airfoil selection is considered a black art by most pilots, and countless cautionary tales abound of the deadly results lurking for the unwary or the bold who dare tamper with factory airfoils in any way. Consequently, the thought of modifying a factory airfoil simply would not occur to most people. Even if it did, to modify an existing fiberglass airfoil, for most people, would also mean building a complete new set of wings, a task beyond the wherewithal of all but a few. Undaunted, Wil determined on an alternative approach. From his research, he concluded further wind-tunnel testing, subsequent to when the *Libelle* entered production, had produced an airfoil better suited for high-speed flight than the one the *Libelle* was using. Desirous of gaining its benefits, he devised a method of reshaping the *Libelle's* airfoil by building it up to the required new shape. All 102.3 square feet of it. Twice that, actually, since each wing has a top and bottom. In many ways, accomplishing this feat was more difficult than building a wing in female molds from the outside in, as the manufacturers do. There is no way to change a wing profile, as Wil did, without hundreds of hours of painstaking filling, sanding, and checking, then repeating the process, seemingly without end. And in order to be in a position to do any checking at all, Wil had to make a series of shape templates to tolerances of less than 1/1000 of an inch, each template of different shape and size because the *Libelle's* wing tapered continuously from root to tip. Then the sanding! This was not the sort of sanding most of us are familiar with. He wasn't making something so crude as a house; even the finest cabinets have *far* rougher surfaces than tolerable for sailplane wings. His sanding was entirely a hand-sanding process, removing infinitesimal amounts at a time, trying to achieve the same flatness — if not better — on his new airfoil as the factories were able to do with wings pulled directly from molds costing tens of thousands of dollars. Sanding as we know it, compared to airfoil sanding, is like butchery compared to brain surgery!

Upon completion of this massive, tedious, sweaty and painstaking operation, Wil then set out to measure as exactly as he could his new ship's glide performance — a second time! Not trusting the published figures for the *Libelle*, he had already done this once on the ship, before beginning the modifications.

There are two ways to measure flight performance of a sailplane, relatively and absolutely. The *relative* method judges the plane's performance against other ships; this can be done in as simple or as rigorous a manner as the pilot has inclination or resources to do. All sailplane pilots indulge in a form of relative flight tests each time they fly in the vicinity of another sailplane. During competitions, these comparisons are taken very seriously indeed. During local and non-contest flying, such informal comparisons are typically used to establish bragging rights. But *accurate* relative performance testing presupposes one glider whose performance is absolutely known already, and the only way to do that is to measure it directly, anyway! *Catch-22.*

Accurate relative performance testing not being available to him, and informal relative comparisons suiting neither his personality nor test goals, Wil had no recourse but to repeat the *absolute* performance measurements he'd painstakingly done prior to beginning the modifications. The only way for him to do this was to take high tows on very still mornings, when the air was absolutely calm, and accurately fly timed speeds over a known distance while measuring the altitude at the beginning and end of each speed run. Each run had to be repeated multiple times to minimize effects of data scatter caused by timing errors, unsensed atmospheric motion, sticking instruments and other gremlins. Done properly, the work is painstaking: instruments must be calibrated beforehand, changes in air density — which varies with altitude and temperature — must be accounted for, speeds must be precisely held. In essence, Wil performed after work and on weekends what teams of engineers spend their careers doing at Edwards Air Force Base. While not a particularly black art, mumbo jumbo, activity the way his previous airfoil selection work was to most people, performance testing a glider is nevertheless exacting in its nature. And expensive. High tows are not cheap.

Upon completion of his flight tests, which indicated to him he had largely been successful in improving the *Libelle's* performance, Wil went out and flew contests. Although he won some regional contests, he never flew the *Libelle* in a National contest before deciding the performance increment he'd gained was not enough to close the gap between it and later, longer-spanned, Open-Class ships. So he subsequently sold this first "Schuemannized *Libelle*" and purchased a longer-span, Swiss-built *Diamant*. The "Schuemannized *Libelle*" is still flying regional competitions today.

Widgets and Wizardry

Unlike the *Libelle*, Wil's modifications of his *Diamant* were limited to internal rather than externally apparent items. He devised a method of automatically positioning the flaps at their lowest drag setting, regardless of the sailplane's airspeed. Flap positioning is particularly important on sailplanes because, unlike powerplanes which use flaps only for landing (and sometimes, takeoff), sailplane flaps can actually bend upwards — backwards to most power pilots — reducing drag at higher speeds. For lowest drag and best performance, sailplane flaps must be adjusted continuously between thermalling and top speed. Operation of the flaps is the pilot's responsibility, selection of the optimum negative flap position being something of a black art in the absence of accurate, measured data — something not terribly common today — and practically nonexistent in the early '70's. One outcome of Wil's research and development became a flap-control system licensed to Schleicher and used in the design of Gerhard Waibel's World-Championship-winning AS-W 20, of which more than 600 have been built since the mid 1970s.

Part of the additional parachute modification Wil made to the "12" was the mounting of a World War II gun camera in various positions on the plane to film the deployment sequences of both 'chutes; this was long before video cameras were invented. He was seeking an understanding of the forces involved, hoping to comprehend and eliminate the inherent unreliability problems of the factory design. Wil was not prone to taking risks with his sailplanes, and some years later, the author read in the Soaring Society of America's monthly journal of a landing he'd made in the "12" on a high-school athletic field during the course of a Nationals (in which he finished sixth). Few gliders in the world could probably have safely duplicated the feat, as athletic fields are generally bordered by fences and peppered with goal posts. To accomplish it in an AS-W 12, of all ships, was startling.

By the early 1970s, Wil was well into development of a device most people subsequently called a "Schuemann box". Contained within a cylindrical, foam-covered container six inches long and five inches in diameter, attached to the variometer and two pressure-sensing ports on the glider by vinyl tubing, were some mysterious workings which could be felt to vibrate gently if thumped by a fingertip. The whole affair weighed but several ounces. Simply put, the box made the variometer display how fast the *atmosphere* was rising or sinking, and it did this independent of the sailplane's speed, altitude or attitude. Most variometers of the time displayed how fast the *sailplane* was rising or sinking, and, because sailplane sink rates increase at high speeds, they often caused the pilot to miss thermals. When flying fast, the thermals merely showed up as reduced sink instead of the lift they could be if the pilot slowed down. The Schuemann box eliminated this problem by providing accurate and instantly usable information to pilots.

The next logical step after improving the *display* of varios was to improve variometers directly. Variometers of the day suspended their indicating needles on jeweled bearings, which always have some inherent internal friction, typically worsening with age. This slows the instrument's needle movements, often by several seconds. Ideally, the instant the sailplane enters a thermal, the needle should immediately rotate to the full deflection corresponding to the actual thermal strength; if the air is going up at 500 feet per minute (f.p.m.), the needle should instantly point at the "5". If it did, the pilot would have accurate knowledge of the *location,* as well as strength of the thermal, and could rapidly center the plane in the best lift. The effect of needle lag is to lie to the pilot about where the thermal actually is; by the time the needle is showing the strongest lift, the plane may well have flown past it, possibly even back into sink. With small thermals, this makes the pilot's job particularly difficult. Trying to compensate for the effects of imperfect instrumentation, experienced pilots would often use the seat of their pants almost as much as the variometer, to tell them how best to center a thermal. Having lesser skills, students and newer pilots generally rely on the variometer. Paradoxically, the pilots who needed good instrumentation the most, often had the worst, since training and club ships of the day endemically had ho-hum instrument systems.

Wil developed a family of variometers, all of which suspended the needle at the center of a twisted band of fine metal ribbon. It operated much like a child's play toy with a button hung at the center of a looped piece of string. Pulling the ends of the string makes the button rotate one direction; relaxing makes it rotate the opposite direction. Using this design, the slowest of Wil's variometers was nearly twice as fast in its needle response as any other mechanical variometer on the market at the time. They were also much more rugged. His top-of-the-line vario actually contained two variometers in one, the smaller, second needle displaying the *average* climb rate achieved in the thermal. This is an important piece of information needed by sailplane pilots, which they would otherwise have to estimate or compute by using a stop watch and altimeter. Estimating is often terribly inaccurate, while timing diverts attention from actually flying the plane and planning ahead for the next thermal.

Wil — joined now by his son, who was a youngster in the early 1970s — still makes and sells these variometers. At the time the author purchased his *Zuni*, which lacked a decent vario, he treated himself to a Schuemann box and a Schuemann variometer. The box has worked flawlessly for over 13 years; after 10 years the vario developed a small leak, diminishing but not eliminating its usefulness in flight. Finally, tiring of the nuisance value of the malfunctioning unit, the author sent the instrument back for repair, which Wil's son rapidly accomplished.

The Shape of Things to Come

All of these contributions to the sport and its participants would be more than enough for most people to have beside their names, but not yet mentioned is perhaps Wil's most amazing contribution, the Schuemann wing planform. Remember Wil's "12"? As good a plane as it was, it too eventually fell prey to newer and better superships. Just as with the *Libelle*, Wil found himself owning a ship no longer competitive in its racing class. Not wanting to bear the expense of moving up to a newer ship, which itself would need replacement a few years down the road, Wil reasoned he could change the "12" from the Open Class to the 15-Meter Class — if he cut off five feet from each wing! So he did. Not with a hacksaw, of course, but with the awesome, painstaking engineering craftsmanship which the people who knew him had come to expect.

With this "new", 15-meter ship, he knew he was entering uncharted territory. It was significantly heavier than any other in the class, its chopped wing relatively broad and stubby for a glider. Both things suggested it would not climb very well compared to other ships in the 15-Meter Class. Wil hoped its weight would more than compensate when the ship ran between the thermals.

His hopes proved forlorn. He found the ship even worse than theory suggested it should be, and he set about understanding why. After an investigation, the envy of the finest fiction detective, Wil arrived at a wonderfully simple (to him) conclusion. His new, short wings were suffering from a previously unknown drag rise at thermalling speeds. The drag was caused by air not flowing directly from front to back of the wings, as theory and common sense said it did, but — under certain conditions — flowing *perpendicular* to the wing. Amazingly, under certain, transitory conditions, the air flowed from the wingtip all the way along the trailing edge of the wing to the wing root. Generally, these conditions occurred when the "12's" wings worked hard to generate lift, most commonly at slow speeds and when pulling up hard from high speed into a thermal. Not content merely to understand the problem, Wil set out to fix it. He embarked on another major modification program to the "12." It took him nearly two years.

His method for eliminating the unwanted, draggy, spanwise flow was elegantly simple in theory. And it works! Klaus Holighaus was the first sailplane designer to design a wing from scratch using Wil's theory. (That plane is still the best in its class a decade after its introduction, a span of time almost inconceivable so rapid have been the aerodynamic advances associated with composite designs.) Every other major German sailplane manufacturer soon followed suit.

The "Schuemann planform" evokes ships of the 1930s, with their gracefully birdlike wings. Wil reasoned he could shape the wing in such a manner that pressures trying to make air flow *outward* on the wing would exactly counteract the *inward* forces which caused the drag rise. If properly done, air would then flow straight across the wing from front to back as all theories assumed it did. Not for him the brute force methods like wing tip plates, or inboard plates, called fences. From his studies of birds, he'd concluded he could either bend the leading edge of the wing aft or bend the tip of

the wing up, to accomplish his goal. Working with the "12", his only practical option was to bend the leading edge back, so this is exactly what he did. In essence, he had to rebuild the outer eight feet of each wing, including the ailerons, which had to be slightly swept back. When finally complete, he had one of the most potent, 15-Meter-Class ships around. He also lost interest in racing — and soaring — about that time!

No Big Deal . . .

Although no longer devoting his considerable talents exclusively toward the sport of soaring, Wil Schuemann's legacy is comprehensive beyond even most soaring pilots' knowledge. A casual trip to almost any gliderport in the U.S. will provide visible proof, whether it be a glider with a Schuemann wing planform, a Schuemann box lurking within the instrumentation innards, or a Schuemann variometer peering forth from the instrument panel. You may even see a Schuemannized *Libelle*. And yet, as remarkable a person as he is for the scope and technical brilliance of his works, he is but one of thousands who have poured effort — and, yes, love — into the sport. The author's *Zuni's* other variometer was designed and built by one of his current club's founders and longtime member, Richard Ball. The *Zuni's* trailer was designed and built by George Applebay, again. The building in which his club keeps community equipment was designed and built by a member, who also donated the building materials. Dr. Kuettner regularly attends his club's monthly meetings and generously gives talks with only a little arm-twisting.

And the author's current club is in no way unique in this regard. Over the years, as a member of clubs in three states and observer of more, each club he's seen has been graced by remarkable people. Beyond the common bond of soaring, shared by each club member, is invariably something more substantial. Entrepreneurs, artists, teachers, engineers, business people, sculptors, photographers, sales people, family people — every individual has often-hidden talents, pursued as enthusiastically and dedicatedly as they pursue their soar-

ing avocations.

Perhaps most remarkable, the vast majority of these people would be genuinely embarrassed at the suggestion their contributions to the sport are noteworthy in any way. While hardly a reason the author became a participant in the sport, over the years he has discovered the vast majority of fellow participants are the sort of people he would want as friends. Happily, many of them are.

There are few other activities about which he can so unreservedly make the same claim.

Chapter Ten

Wilderness Doug

Outlandings are inevitable for the serious soaring pilot, since, no matter how great one's experience and soaring skills, the weather can always generate a new surprise. Early in training, the aspiring sailplane pilot usually begins to learn the dreaded truth: Fly a glider long enough, and you eventually won't get back to the airport. For most, learning that a day will come when they more or less *willingly* prepare to land an engineless airplane at an unfamiliar airport or —*horrors!* — some farmer's field miles from any pavement, doesn't deter their quest to master engineless flight. Admittedly, most student pilots begin to consider the possibility with heightened awareness, once it's pointed out to them! And only the foolhardy thirst for their initial outlandings before completing extensive preparations. They questioned instructors and fellow pilots, absorbed the literature, practiced field selection from the air with later follow-up by car, practiced landings with covered altimeter and became proficient at touching down within a few feet of their selected aiming point at the proper speed. So, by the time most pilots actually make their first outlanding, the event is less an emergency requiring Divine intervention than it is just another task for which they've prepared and been trained. Nevertheless, landing in a field always contains an element of risk beyond that of a landing back at the airport from which the pilot towed. The first off-airport landing results in the same sweaty palms as the first solo. Perhaps sweatier. The intellectual fact others have safely done it before, is no comfort when you are circling slowly down, in dead air, trying to pick the field least likely to cause harm to your precious craft. All the book knowledge in the world can't compare to the real thing!

Somewhere in the final 1,500 feet above the touchdown, you accept the fact that a landing in some field is inevitable. With this acceptance comes a slight reduction of tension, as if the mind/body system knows it can better concentrate on the all-important task of flying safely if it isn't fixated nervously on trying to avoid the inevitable. The earlier in the landing pattern you experience this slight relaxation of stress, the better you normally do.

Nevertheless, if you're ever present to see a glider landing in a field, watch the pilot closely after the plane stops rolling. It matters not whether the landing is his first or his one-hundred-and-first, the very first thing he or she will do after stepping from the cockpit is get down on hands and knees and inspect the underside of the airplane! If you had a remote heart monitor you'd also see a distinctly elevated heart rate. Only the foolhardy, or utterly resigned, don't consider outlandings a wonderful focuser of thought! Additionally, they're something of an emotional roller coaster. Stampeding in close order are depression, anxiety and elation: depression at the unsuccessful completion of the flight task; anxiety about the forthcoming outlanding; elation in its safe aftermath.

Very occasionally, you do everything almost exactly right only to discover you've overlooked something important. Such was the case for Wilderness Doug.

Walden is roughly in the center of North Park, Colorado. A "park" in the intermountain west refers to a valley surrounded by mountains. Sometimes the term "hole" is used, instead, hence Estes Park and Jackson Hole. Approximately

40 miles long and half that in width, North Park's axis flows north and south some 8,100 feet above sea level. The southern and western borders of the valley are the mountains which form the Continental Divide. To the east, curving in a northwesterly direction in a nearly unbroken arc, are the Medicine Bow Mountains. Beyond the Medicine Bows are more — lower — mountains to the north, east and south. These roll toward Laramie forty miles into the Laramie Valley to the northeast, and terminate at the Great Plains just west of Fort Collins the same distance east. With the exception of the alpine Medicine Bow Mountains, the heavily forested hilltops east of Walden are generally below timberline and sparsely populated. The few roads there are dirt, tending to follow glacially carved water courses.

The Medicine Bow region of Colorado is one of the state's better kept, dramatic secrets. Though the mountain range lacks a dominating peak, it makes up for the omission with a nearly unbroken, 40-mile spine of gray rock, almost entirely above 12,000 feet, chiseling into the sky. This rugged and dramatic ridgeline has surrendered to man's roads in but two places: Cameron Pass, the southeastern entrance to North Park, and King's Canyon an exit, 30 miles distant to the northeast. The aeronautical charts show only one nearby small hamlet east of the Medicine Bows — Glendevey. It is situated at the eastern base of the Medicine Bows, so far away from both landable fields and what passes for population centers in this part of Colorado that few sailplane pilots actually know where it is. Glendevey is, in fact, a crossroads, not a village.

The group of sailplane pilots gathering at Walden, in August of 1986, gave no thought to Glendevey or any other point east of the Medicine Bows. They thought, instead, to enjoy soaring for a long weekend above North Park. Assembled for the camp were some seven or eight privately-owned gliders, a club's Schweizer 1-34 and the club's towplane. One of the privately-owned ships was a partnership, an ideal situation for Doug — the only partner flying at this camp.

The camp began — as all camps must — with the ritual

of glider assembly. As usual, there was a certain urgency to
the task, as, until everything is assembled, checked, and
equipment properly stowed, there can be no opportunity to
go soaring regardless of how fine the weather. The early
clouds gave indication of a strong southwesterly wind aloft;
the westerlies, which tend to dominate Colorado's weather
spring and fall, were working. Hopes for good ridge lift on
the Medicine Bows, a scant 12 miles downwind of the airport, were expressed.

Following the mid-morning urgent bustle of rigging
gliders, a strange calm descended as prospective pilots immediately switched to attentive waiting. No one wanted to
tow too early and not be able to remain aloft, yet none
wanted to miss any possible soaring! Falling out is not only
an unwanted expense, it also drains some of the creative
energies so helpful to making the most of soaring conditions. Adding to the difficulty of deciding when to take the
first tow is the wind. It had scoured down to ground level
before noon, and was blowing 20 miles per hour at an angle
to the runway. The crosswind made takeoffs and landings
potentially more difficult. Wind also tends to disrupt thermals, and, in the mountains, always portends turbulence
below peak levels. Some wind is normal; too much is dis-
couraging, particularly before the first guinea pig takes to
the skies!

After a delay of several hours, the windblown cumulus clouds were just too inviting to ignore. More experienced pilots began launching first. Those still on the ground
could see and hear on the radio how others were doing.
Conditions were boisterous but good. Launches proceeded
steadily. Pilots discussed the conditions.

"Have you seen the 1-34 lately?" asked one.

A look skyward. "No, not for the last hour. Last I knew,
he was reporting thirteen thousand feet, four miles east of
the field."

The unspoken concern behind the question was for the
club member flying the 1-34. The plane was not only the low-
est-performance glider of the single seaters at the camp, the

pilot had expressed a desire to fly it the 73 air miles back to Boulder, rather than trailer it. Would he attempt it on this daunting a day?

"Tell you what. Loser mows around the winner's trailer; I'll bet you he doesn't land back at this airport," smirked the first pilot.

His friend looked again at the sky, briefly reconsidering a conversation held the previous evening with the present pilot of the 1-34. He grinned in reply, "No bet."

Shortly thereafter, the first pilot tried again. "I'll bet Doug doesn't make it back either!"

"You're on," said his friend, believing it was a sucker bet all the way.

Doug, while reasonably new to soaring, in general, and to mountain soaring, in particular, seemed to combine a healthy sense of self-preservation with cautious good judgment.

They sealed the bet, knowing it wasn't about five minutes of mowing weeds but an indirect reflection of the by now thoroughly unpleasant wind conditions. It was a reminder between friends to not do anything stupid when their turn to soar.

Several hours later, the pilot who chose Doug's side of the bet landed, and he was helped by his friend to disassemble in the worsening winds. Because he could see the 1-34 safely resting on its trailer, he presumed Doug's ship was also in its trailer. Against the wind, he shouted, "Thanks for the help, Dick! And thanks for the mow job, too!"

Dick gave him an odd look, shouting back, "Doug landed out!"

"Really?" So Doug had his first off-field landing under his belt. Good for him! Almost as a polite afterthought he asked, "Are he and the plane okay?"

"Yes. The plane's not damaged, and he's all right."

Priorities one and two.

Then, "So how come his trailer's still here? Where is he?"

"He landed in a field east of the Medicine Bows . . ."

Ugh. A long retrieve.

". . . and we're trying to figure out where the nearest road is. In fact, he landed in a wilderness area, and there aren't any nearby roads!"

It seems Doug, along with Dick and three other gliders including the 1-34, had all been soaring in the strong ridge and thermal lift along the peaks of the Medicine Bows, *down-wind* of the airport. Nevertheless, the 1-34 had gotten back, so conditions had obviously been good enough to warrant soaring there. Plus, Doug's German-built Grob *Astir CS* was a much better penetrator than the 1-34, and they all had working radios. *Perhaps*, his stunned friend thought, *flying there had been a group decision.* Regardless, it would be a while before Doug could answer everyone's questions.

"Tom is trying to cross the Medicine Bows right now in a four-wheel drive with the county Sheriff. Judy, Sharon and Dave are in town trying to arrange for an air drop of supplies to him."

No new information was available for the next several hours. Supplies were found to enable the towplane to ferry a care package to Doug. Two bundles were made from the group's supplies. In one was high-energy food, heavy outer clothing and a sleeping bag. The other contained Dave's tent. Doug's position on the map was but 13 air-miles from the Walden airport; another glider pilot was the first to relay radio messages from the downed plane, easily visible from aloft. The four-wheel drive expedition returned with long faces. Not only were there no tracks even remotely suitable for these vehicles, but the federal government, in the form of the U.S. Forest Service, had begun to let it be known it would make no difference. No motorized vehicles are permitted into wilderness areas. All waited for the towplane to return.

Short minutes after departing, the club's 180-hp Super Cub was sighted descending from the east. Dave wasted no time landing and tying down. He and his wife, Sharon — acting as crew chief — made but one drop run, ejecting both parcels on Dave's command, battered by horrendously violent sink. For an awful moment, Dave thought the sink was

going to swat the tug into the treetops. Doug saw both packages tumble down, but he never found the tent. His landout expenses had begun.

Unable to do anything else for him that evening, the group retired to dinner, and the conversation centered on Doug. They knew all was fine but the retrieve arrangements; fellowship among friends soon returned. Gallows humor eased their tensions. The last pilot to see Doug on the ridge reported that one second he'd been with them at 15,000 feet, well above the ridge line, and the next he was not. An hour later someone heard his radio call from the ground.

The next morning — Sunday — most of the group did what any self-respecting friends of a healthy downed glider pilot would do, go soaring! But not before arranging with an outfitter from Glendevey to ride in on horseback and pick up Doug. One pilot volunteered to retrieve Doug that afternoon rather than going flying. The 13 air miles translated into nearly 60 road miles, the last half of which were dirt. The roads wended down one side of the Medicine Bows, across 10,276-foot-high Cameron Pass, then back up a glacial valley, completely carpeted in mature pine trees all the way to Glendevey. The few rocky pastures visible from the car were more than 15 miles from the head of the valley. All had difficult landing approaches blocked by hillsides, electric wires or fencing.

Glendevey itself apparently consisted of a single, well kept ranch. Visible was a log horse barn, log bunk house for the hands, log lodge and split-rail fencing enclosing a corral and several pastures. No vehicles or people were in sight. No vehicles had been passed on the way in. No smoke rose from the cookhouse chimney. Doug's crew parked the car near the cookhouse, "Halloing" as he opened the door. The smell of fresh brownies was overwhelming. An attractive young woman in her early twenties stepped from behind the massive fireplace dominating a portion of the room, smiling in greeting, as if strangers routinely walked in uninvited. This was Kristin Peterson, son of Garth, proprietor of the ranch. Although a working ranch, dude ranch vacationers and hunt-

ers were also welcomed.

Ninety minutes later, the nicker of horses in the corral, greeting returning animals, heralded the return of her father — the rescue party — and Doug. The need to retrieve the glider by helicopter was discussed, and permission to use one of their corrals as a heliport was given with polite equanimity, as if the Peterson's daily experienced such odd requests.

Doug had been flying in boisterous lift created by tons and tons of air deflected upward as it crossed the Medicine Bow's ridgeline. With the others, he'd cruised on a line extending from Cameron Pass at the south end of the ridge to another, lower area northeast of the Walden airport. In the loose company of four other gliders, it had been an opportunity for everyone to enjoy 30 miles of uninterrupted ridge cruising — stick the nose down and run long distances at high speeds kind of soaring — something relatively rare in the jumbled mountain ranges of the west. The opportunity was too tempting to ignore, despite the ridge's location downwind of the airport. He'd even reassured himself he could penetrate back upwind to the airport, by actually doing it once, before committing to ridge soaring the Medicine Bows. He'd subsequently made two trips along the peaks. Then, on one leg to Cameron Pass and for reasons he couldn't explain, rather than reversing direction for the return trip by banking to the right — upwind, away from the ridge — Doug turned left. In the 30 seconds it took for the plane's nose to curve, first through south then east and finally through north and back around west, he drifted from his vantage point, 1,000 feet directly atop the ridge, to half a mile east — downwind — of the ridge line. The surging buoyancy of moments before was replaced by the feel of straps pressing into his shoulders as the plane accelerated down toward the east side of the ridge slope, trapped now in crushing sink. There was no escape.

He was sinking far too fast to fly the half mile upwind to the safety of the west side of the ridge; he would have crashed

into the east face of the Medicine Bows. Directly below and behind him was nothing but the bristling blackness of pine trees, thrashing in the torrents of air swirling in the upper reaches of the glacial valley.

The shocking change in his circumstances was accompanied by instant, daunting turbulence. Loose equipment, dirt and dust floated, slithered and scratched all around him in a concert of stress. The *Astir* creaked and popped, pulling G's in the maelstrom, all despite no control inputs from Doug. It was all he could do to keep the plane on an even keel. He'd never experienced anything like it, neither the turbulence nor the grasping trees beckoning his crash. He would later realize he was nearly in tears in his desperation to escape. Despite the terror, despite the difficulty in maintaining control — despite everything — something in his makeup and training still worked, though, however unconsciously. That *something* directed him to do the only thing which *might* save him from an immediate, life-threatening crash. His one choice, to delay the inevitable, was to allow himself to drift even *farther* downwind toward the eastern slopes of the glacial valley. This he did, perhaps instinctively sensing that only there might this torrent of down be deflected upward again in its mad rush for the plains. Later, he was unable to describe the relief he experienced upon feeling the first upward surge; at that moment, for the first time since his ill-advised downwind turn above the distant ridgeline mere moments ago, he had his first faint hopes for his future.

Trapped there, in the roiling turbulence of the glacial valley, able to delay the sickeningly, mind-numbingly, inevitable, while still unable to see a way out of his dilemma, Doug's mind slowly began functioning again. He decided if he was to have a chance for a safe landing, there was but one possible way out. He could not go back west across the ridge — now thousands of feet above him — for there was nothing in the aerial maelstrom to carry him aloft. South was out due to high mountains. He briefly considered continuing east across the lower crests of the foothills, but the prospect of 30 miles of tree-covered, unknown terrain deterred him. He could only fly north, toward the lower end of the glacial valley. It was, he rationalized, also closer to Walden. Looking down the valley, he saw nothing but a U-shaped channel carpeted thickly with pines. In a place or two, a dirt road could be seen peeking from beneath the pines; apparently, it followed the contours of the valley. He was nearly at the bottom of that channel, barely 200 feet above the thrashing boughs. Never before from an airplane had he been able to see pine trees blowing in the wind.

I must really be in trouble! came the rhetorical thought. Casting it aside, with the grim determination of a man without hope, he began extending his despairing circles to the north, expecting at any second to feel the sickening drop which would accompany his final plunge toward the treetops.

Circling as close to the canyon's west-facing, east wall as he dared in the turbulence, he found he could just barely husband his altitude cushion as he felt his way down the valley. Here a surge of lift, there wild sink. All the time, ceaseless violence. Fortunately, the valley sloped down faster then he was losing altitude, and five minutes later he estimated the valley floor was now several hundred feet farther away from him. Unfortunately, it had begun to level out with no place yet to land. Without a thermal, he was still going to crash.

The valley had widened in his journey north; ice in eons past had scraped more of the rocks away. Farther now from the Medicine Bows looming to his west, the turbulence seemed less vicious in the widening valley. Forcing himself to remain calm, drawing upon his training and experience, and summoning from within a courage born of desperation, in the next roiled boost of lift, he rolled into as steep a turn as he dared, trying to fly it like he would a real thermal. Never before had he concentrated so fiercely on maintaining a coordinated turn. The slightest stall, the slightest uncoordination could instantly become a low-altitude spin in the ragged air. Then there would truly be no hope. Working desperately to maintain safe airspeed, a coordinated turn and the steep bank, and fighting against the constant upsets and changes thrown him by the winds, he began climbing! For the first time in 15 minutes. It was an anemic little climb, but to Doug it was also a major triumph. It proved he *could* climb in this wild air. Ultimately, it provided another 600 feet of ground clearance, practically double what he'd had when the climb began.

Losing the lift, he glided farther north, then wrenched the *Astir* into another sweating bank. This thermal was a good one! Soon he found himself approaching 13,000 feet — higher than the Medicine Bows now several miles to his west. He spotted some pastures in the valley, the first possible landing sites he'd seen since falling into this trap. He could even practically see Walden! And now, perched safely, high above the glacial valley, his goal seemingly almost in hand, Doug succumbed to the disease of "Get-home-itis". When the thermal quit at 13,100 feet, he immediately banked the nose of the *Astir* west — upwind, toward the barrier of the Medicine Bows — seeking to cross them while he had the altitude. It was hopeless. Though not four miles away, he instantly found himself caught, once again, in the grasp of endless, crushing sink; he made miserable progress against the fierce wind. Within minutes he was once again at 10,200 feet, barely above the valley floor, and once again without a landable field in reach. Berating himself as he sought to drift back to the east side of the valley, he pledged to himself to climb higher next time . . . to give himself a fighting chance.

Another roiled bubble, another drift north. Finally, he found himself at 13,200 feet, once again within reach of several pastures. But here, though now five miles from the Medicine Bows, the alpine barrier was cleft by a low notch, Ute Pass. All he had to do was clear *it* and he would be out of this hell hole and safe. He would be *home!*

Above a dirt crossroads, he extracted his map and thought. One road led west to Glendevey at the base of the Medicine Bows before turning northward again, the other road continued north up the east side of the quickly widening valley. Both rejoined in another 10 miles. He'd reached the mouth of the glacial valley. He was now at an upper reach of one arm of the huge Laramie Valley. He'd safely flown the most difficult 20 miles of his life. Laramie's huge concrete airport was now another 50 distant, beyond completely unfamiliar terrain. Wisely, he ruled out making an attempt for Laramie as foolish under the circumstances. Seduced by the nearness of the pass, using a hayfield in the main valley below as his first "out" and what appeared to be a pasture on the west side of an intermediate ridge between him and Ute Pass as his second "out," he turned west toward Glendevey.

Lured by the tantalizing proximity of the pass, bolstered by the new plan in his mind, buoyed by the essence of a suddenly promising outlook for his immediate future, he flew with a renewed sense of purpose. It seemed *possible*. Nose down to pick up the speed needed to penetrate into the teeth of the wind, he began his second attempt to recross the Medicine Bows. For the first few minutes, despite slow progress, his hopes rose as he maintained altitude, encountering neither lift nor sink. *If this keeps up just a little longer, I can make it!* he thought. His judgment clouded by stress and hope, Doug now made his second major mistake. As he neared the ranch, he encountered light sink. Expecting it, and counting on lift on the west side of the intervening ridge, he pressed on, not unduly concerned. Then, surprisingly to him, his precious altitude began evaporating rapidly as he overflew the ranch, nearing the small ridge beyond. Still expecting lift beyond the ridge, he continued. Finally, atop the crest of the ridge, still in strong sink, expecting lift that could not be, he realized — too late! — he was committed once more to a course of action with a doubtful future. Safe altitude to make a 180° turn had vanished. His heart in his mouth, now, he searched frantically for the pasture he'd seen from afar. *It had disappeared!*

He was stunned. Surely he'd seen a field here just minutes before. *What in the world?* Then, just as suddenly, he deduced the problem: he was *so* low the pasture was hidden by the tops of the trees ahead! It had to be there, it just *had* to be. Fortunately, the ground beyond the crest now sloped away from him as he searched anxiously for the vanished pasture. Down below a normal pattern altitude, he finally saw it ahead and to his right. It was frighteningly short, but he had no more choices! Now, urgently, he lowered the gear, repositioned his hands on stick and spoiler controls. Fighting low-altitude turbulence he banked right, waited until almost in line with the long axis of the pasture, corrected left one last time, then concentrated on clearing the tree tops as low as he dared. When the treeline rushed beneath the leading edge of the wing behind his shoulders, he opened full spoilers to get down before he ran out of field. The instant he descended below the trees, the bottom dropped out beneath him, spoilers taking effect the same instant most of his headwind vanished. As the sailplane fell toward the unyielding ground, he desperately slammed the spoilers shut, pulled back on the stick to get the proper fuselage angle for landing, waited a moment and eased the spoilers open again. Suddenly, startlingly, vision blurring as the wheel contacted the uneven ground, he bounced once, then was down and rolling. He hauled on the spoiler handle with all his might, desperately seeking as much braking action as possible before the wheel dropped into an animal burrow and tore off the landing gear, or he crashed into the trees ahead. Finally, in an instant that lasted a lifetime, the noise and vibration stopped. A wingtip dropped in slow motion to the ground. It had been one hour since he'd turned left atop the Medicine Bows.

After hours of wind hissing past the canopy, hours filled first with the simple pleasures of mountain soaring, then with an almost incomprehensible violence, tension, fear and stress, the silence was unsettling. Then, gradually, the sounds of earth returned as he sat in the cockpit collecting his thoughts and trying to relax. Something, though, wasn't right. As he opened the canopy he heard the snuffling of large animals. Looking around he was alarmed to see a small herd of cattle approaching, their curiosity overcoming startlement and fear. His heart sank; stories of cattle damaging gliders by using them as salt licks and back scratchers are oft told among soaring pilots. Not knowing what else to do, he undid his seat belts and parachute straps and clambered out. The instant he stood upright, the lead cattle, semi-wild range creatures that they were, stopped in alarm, sniffed suspiciously then wheeled as one and broke for the trees. With a sigh of relief, and unable to control his bursting curiosity, Doug fell on hands and knees to inspect the belly of the _Astir_, half sick of what he might find. To his immense relief, the plane appeared undamaged. He rocked back onto his heels with another sigh, wiped his brow with a forearm, stood slowly and surveyed his field for the first time. Ahead, in a narrowing vee, the pasture ended at the trees he'd braked so vigorously to avoid. As his gaze swept the full perimeter of the pasture, his heart began to sink once more. Nowhere could he see signs of a road. He set out to pace off the dimensions of his field; perhaps an aero retrieve? According to the altimeter, the field was at 9,500 feet; according to his feet, it was only 650 feet by 750 feet along its major axes; according to his eyes it was surrounded by 50-foot-tall pine trees. No aero retrieve.

He looked at his watch; it was 3:15 PM. Overhead, the sun blazed from an azure sky. Above his green prison the wind still ripped at the tree tops, belying the warm serenity at ground level. He needed help, and he knew it. Perhaps one of pilots still flying along the Medicine Bows could somehow help him by radio relay. Shaking his head in growing dejection, he reached for the radio. . .

At 6:00 P.M., Doug snapped off the radio to conserve battery power. There was nothing more to be done; the last glider was landing at Walden. He would have to spend the night here in Shipman Park within the Rawah Wilderness area. _It's ironic_, he thought, _some people work very hard to enjoy the serenity of the wilderness experience . . . and what a pretty place this would be, if only my glider wasn't here._ Shadows lengthened from the western trees; they would soon reach the airplane. By then he was certain he would have to walk out, for no four-wheel-drive access trails came within miles of the spot. The question was, walk to where? He would learn the answer in 15 hours; they'd scheduled another radio conference at 9:00 AM. In the meantime, he was on his own.

Soon, dusk began casting a purple cloak over the pasture. He rested in the cockpit, thinking. This had been a day filled with once-in a-lifetime — he hoped! — experiences, many of them unpleasant, and, in a sense, the stress was far from over. He reflected on the morning so filled with camaraderie and promise. Ridge soaring as he'd never before experienced. Then, *The Turn.* Always. . . The Turn. It gnawed at him. Next, the endless scratching flight down the death-filled valley. The unexpected hope of the pass. And now this, an interminable night leading into an uncertain future.

Helpless to stop them, his thoughts raced in a mad, churning jumble in silent emulation of the air above. At first he'd busied himself in physical activity: securing the plane with his tiedown kit; retrieving the clothing and food his friends had flown in; searching unsuccessfully for the second bundle. He owed someone a tent, he realized; that would be one of the cheaper expenses of this retrieve. He'd forced himself to eat something, anything, knowing his system needed it; the food practically stuck in his throat. Reading proved hopeless, he couldn't concentrate. Frustrated, anxious, apprehensive and wired, he'd finally retreated to the haven provided by the cockpit. He'd better get used to it; it would be his tent. His thoughts continued their mad race.

Will I get out of this alive? How? It's a good thing Mom and Dad still live in Florida, they never were too keen on my soaring. Am I really going to need a helicopter to retrieve the plane? Are there bears in a wilderness area? Mountain Lions? Why did I ever make that turn?! Why didn't I turn back by that ranch? Should I even be flying a sailplane? Am I dangerous? What will I do if those cattle return? What are cattle doing in a wilderness area, anyway?! Will they keep wild animals away or do they attract predators? I wonder what Dick and the rest of the crew are doing at this instant? Man, I've really thrown everybody a monkey wrench. I guess someday I'll have to tell Mom and Dad, if the embarrassment of it all doesn't kill me first. Jeez! How did I ever manage to do this?!? Oh man, oh man . . .

His night lasted 72 hours. Never had the cockpit been so

uncomfortable — lumps and jabs came from everywhere. It got cold, despite the down jacket Dave had dropped. Each time he snapped it on to sweep its pitifully small glow outside the canopy, he wondered if the flashlight's batteries would last the night. How were the wild animals smart enough to remain just beyond its reach? In between the cold, the discomfort and the fear, time passed in painfully small chunks; at times he dozed. He finally fell into a fitful sleep of exhaustion; he awakened when the gray of false dawn lighted the eastern sky two hours later. He felt completely unrested. He was still alone; there were no paw marks, claw marks or other mystery marks on the canopy. There were no cattle. Today, he would be rescued, but another lifetime would first have to pass before he learned how.

Five minutes early, he gratefully turned on the *Astir's* radio again. Promptly at 9:00 A.M., tinny words shattered the mountain silence.

"Golf Six, Eight-Five Fox."

"Go ahead, Eight-Five Fox."

"Ahh . . . good morning, Doug." He recognized Dave's voice again. "We've arranged for a trail guide from Glendevey to pack in and get you out. That's all we could think of to do. He hit the trail around seven; should be there by nine-thirty or ten, they said. Over."

"Understood, Dave. Thanks. I guess I'll see you later today, then?"

"Roger. Someone will drive around to pick you up. Anything else to report? How was your night?"

"Ahhh . . . I've had better . . . Uh . . . Golf Six out, I guess."

"Eight-Five Fox out."

Doug snapped off the radio once more, his waiting tinged for the first time with anticipation and nervousness.

At 10:30 A.M., resting in the shade of the wing with his back against the fuselage, Doug contemplated his surroundings. Except for the indentations of cattle, some cow pies and a long-overgrown jeep track, he could be the first human in this spot. He and his space ship. The cattle had not returned.

His was a world of birds and imagined animals in the woods. Earlier, with each popping twig, his imagination helped some time pass. Now, he was in a state closer to meditation. The vibrations of hooves thudding nearby didn't intrude until the stranger was less than 20 feet away, behind him. He looked over his shoulder, across the top of the fuselage. A man — a cowboy actually — sat astride a large horse, looking around. Another horse followed behind, tethered to the saddle horn of the cowboy's mount. Feeling awkward, not wanting to startle the horses, Doug cleared his throat. When the man looked his way, Doug spoke. "You're probably looking for me…"

"Howdy, I'm Garth Peterson. Your friends said I could expect to find you here," the cowboy said evenly.

In contrast to the interminable preceding 24 hours, the rest of his second day flew by in an instant: the horseback ride to Glendevey, the drive back to Walden, where camp was being broken as people began the metamorphosis from glider camp participants to their working worlds. Soon, the airport was deserted but for two cars and two glider trailers, one empty. For his crew, the vacant airport had the sweet-sad, empty air of good times recently ended; for Doug, the busy afternoon still held multiple phone calls and talks with various government agencies — police, sheriff, U.S. Forest Service — to verify that the emergency was over. Then a new series of phone calls designed to obtain permission to bring a motorized vehicle — the helicopter! — into a wilderness area. Of course, he would also have to locate a helicopter company. Potential major hurdles, both.

By 8:15 P.M., everything seemed all set except for government approval; the person who could give it couldn't be located at the late hour. They can do no more that night.

Monday, 1:45 P.M., Glendevey Lodge. After a morning of additional phone calls, Doug and crew arrived; a note instructed them to make themselves at home until Garth returned. Life at the lodge went on at its normal rhythm as if they were not there.

Garth returns; by 2 P.M., all was ready but the helicopter.

At 2:50 P.M. . . . the sound of a truck growling its way closer intruded on the pastoral setting. Saying, "That must be the fuel truck," Doug walked around the building to await its arrival. Soon, a dual-wheel pickup truck with a gleaming, cream-colored fuel tank in its bed pulled around by his trailer. The driver, a lanky, dark-haired man wearing a baseball cap, stepped out, grinning.

"Hi! This must be the place!"

"I reckon. Have any trouble finding us?"

"Nope. You're quite a ways in, though. Took me nearly three hours to get here. The chopper guys probably stopped back at the shop for lunch between jobs. Should be here soon." He pulled a piece of straw and chewed on it.

Minutes after the truck's arrival, three heads snapped up as the radio crackled, "Can you hear us yet?"

The truck driver retrieved a radio. "Not yet."

"We're less than five out."

Five miles, five minutes, it doesn't matter. They were close, but the wind carried the sound away. Not as strong as it had been the previous three days, it was still blowing 15 m.p.h. at ground level . . . twice that in thermal gusts. Then, suddenly, from the southeast, the unmistakable whine of a turbine-powered helicopter. Leaning across the fence, Doug and crew watched as seconds later the bubble of a modified Bell 47 helicopter approaching low over the trees — the type used on *M*A*S*H* — appeared. It settled gently to earth 50 feet from fence and trailer. Between the grass of the pasture and the wind, the arrival was as undramatic as a helicopter arrival can be. There was no dust, the wind carried the outflow from its blades away from the few spectators, the horses in the nearby corral paid little attention.

Helicopter and glider crews convened by a split-rail fence for a strategy session. The plan soon became for Doug and the sling load pilot to chopper in to derig the glider; the ferry pilot, fuel driver and Doug's crew would handle operations at the lodge. Safety regulations prohibited anyone but the pilot to be onboard when the helicopter had a sling load beneath it. The chopper crew, a congenial lot, quickly laid out the sling beside the chopper, placed within it the derigging hardware Doug had prepared, attached the sling to a hook on a side mount. Looking something like a ship's ladder, roughly square in shape when laid flat, the sling was attached at each corner to a stout, 100-foot-long, rope-like affair, the other end of which snapped into a hook on the side of the chopper. The entire load could be instantly dumped by the pilot if safety demanded. Ducking beneath the open side of the plexiglass, Doug entered the right seat of the chopper, the sling pilot climbed in the other side.

The retrieve proved anticlimactic. Four helicopter trips later, the *Astir* is cocooned safely within its trailer. Hands were shaken all around, Doug and crew expressed heartfelt thanks to the helicopter men, who, in their opinion, had only been doing their jobs. Still, they'd done so professionally, competently and, most of all, safely. Incredibly, throughout the entire ordeal, the plane suffered no damage at all, as a subsequent inspection by a professional airplane mechanic confirmed. It was almost too much to be believed. Doug's first landout was now history.

The rest of the retrieve? Compared to what he'd just experienced, retrieving the fender which fell off his trailer, then sweating fuel to the only gas station open for miles around at 10:30 at night were trivial! Doug dropped his crew off at the paved road where they'd left his car and trailer. They convoyed down Poudre Canyon to the gas station, where they went their separate ways. Doug wasn't seen at the airport for approximately one month.

Word of the helicopter retrieve spread rapidly. People asked Doug's crew about it each time he went to the airport to fly.

"Ask Doug," he replied to all.

Prior to helping with the retrieve, Doug had been an acquaintance — albeit a friendly one — he'd met through soaring; he wasn't a close friend. And although worried what effect the experience would have on him as a pilot, the crew didn't feel it was his place to call and pester Doug to return to the cockpit. But after such a traumatic experience, he wondered if Doug would stick with the sport. Essentially he'd made but two mistakes: the initial downwind turn when atop the Medicine Bows and the ill-advised pressing on beyond the ridge west of Glendevey, guaranteeing a risky landout. Landing in a Wilderness Area had simply been an unlucky break. The rest of the time he'd done very well, indeed.

There's a saying in the flying community which goes: *When the going gets tough, you won't rise to the occasion, you will default to the level of your training.* It reflects the often grim humor of pilots who know better than anyone that mistakes can kill. Even your life being on the line isn't immunization against stupidity, lack of training, or panic. In a critical, life threatening situation, Doug hadn't panicked. He'd had the training and levelheadedness to enable him to survive a desperate situation without damage or harm. His crew hoped he would stick with the sport.

About a month later, one fine fall morning, Doug's crew learned of his decision. While assembling his own plane, he saw Doug's unmistakable red pickup drive to the airport gate. At the first chance, he strolled over to Doug, now standing by the *Astir's* fuselage. "Going flying?"

"Yeah, I think so," Doug said, straightening from fiddling in the cockpit, gazing toward the western sky. "This'll be the first time since my landout, too." He paused. "Hope I do better this time." He wore a new T-shirt, a gift from his fiancée. On his chest, emblazoned in black and red across the brilliant yellow T-shirt, were the words: **Wilderness Doug . . . Yeah, I'm the one!**

Chapter Eleven

Reflections

Every profession, every avocation, has its war stories . . . tales of sometimes questionable provenance linked by one unvarying thread. Namely, the listener is thankful he or she wasn't the subject of the story! Flying, and soaring, is no different. Happily, bad luck of the kind which snared Wilderness Doug is rare. In his 20-plus years of soaring, most of the author's experiences have been far more pleasant. And, in time, Wilderness Doug learned to view his experience with less immediacy and more perspective. He continues to enjoy the sport a wiser, more reflective individual.

The fact is, few who participate in soaring find themselves unchanged by their participation. For to realize the dream of flying with the birds inexorably gives all who do a new perspective on their world, a perspective which molds their very being. To do things like this: to climb 6,000 feet up a cloud canyon at dusk surrounded by a hundred shades of gray, a thousand pinks and violets — from the faintest lilac to a vivid purplescent glow, from the lightest rose to an erubescent crimson; to see countless nuances of color, experience startling sensations of structure, depth and tex-

ture lent the scene by fingers of light gleaming past un-
seen crenelations of towering cloud turrets, emerging from
a formless mass of tenebrous clouds separating glider from
sun; to be where nowhere is there the sun, everywhere its
effects; to weave a path through infinite sky in infinitesimal craft toward the fading light, questing after the
uncatchable; to see the cloud crevasse through which you've
climbed fall into final evening shadow, the unfathomably
high wall of western cloud fade to formless, menacing
gloom; to turn your gaze away from the foreboding mass,
to the east beyond the tops of the clouds to distant plains
glowing warm and orange beyond the racing line of the
terminator; to be at 18,000 feet, watching the darkening
world below twinkle into man-made heavens; to land in
twilight, chilled to the bone by early December cold. It's
impossible to do these things and not view the world dif-
ferently than you did before you went aloft.

It's impossible to gaze down from 31,000 feet at a crys-
talline world gone distant and flat and not be humbled.
It's impossible to dance with a sundog for hours along miles
of lenticular cloud and not be exalted.

It's impossible to go from the simple thrill of one's first
sailplane ride to the certainty that *ahead*, or *over there*,
will be found another thermal, to do this again and again
while hundreds of miles sweep beneath you and your sailplane, and not reflect back on how these wonders became
attainable.

It's impossible to expand your thinking until it encom-
passes not just the world around you, but the world *above*,
and not sometimes wonder about who you have become.

To the sailplane pilot, the sky isn't some unfathom-
able mystery to be feared, or cursed at or grumbled about.
It becomes an extension of his world, a part no sailplane
pilot feels quite right without periodically visiting. To soar
with the birds is to *become* part bird. To dance with the
clouds is to appreciate more the ethereal. Not a flight will
pass in which you won't learn something new, whether
about the atmosphere, your ship or yourself.

But no matter how experienced you may become in the aerial arena, though the hours may accumulate, flight distances increase, though you feel more at home in the sky, you are always but a temporary visitor. Once free and soaring, no one will hear your passage, rarely will you be seen, no trace of your journey will linger in the sky. But all the traces will linger within, whispering down the years through those others, all of us granted the privilege to fulfill man's long-held dream to fly with the birds. From Orville, through others known and unknown, their passage allows our passage.

The lure of the sky is universal. Words from an earlier, meaner time still ring through the years. From amidst all the horrors of World War II rose small treasures for its survivors and for posterity, tendrils of life reaching from the void. John Gillespie Magee, a 19-year-old American flying with the Royal Canadian Air Forces who lost his life early in the war when his Spitfire collided with another plane returning from a patrol over the English Channel. He left his spiritual joy as mankind's legacy, expressed in poem. He would have made a fine sailplane pilot.

High Flight

Oh, I have slipped the surly bonds of Earth,
And danced the skies on laughter-silvered wings:
Sunward I've climbed and joined the tumbling mirth
Of sun-split clouds — and done a hundred things
You have not dreamed of — wheeled and soared and swung
High in the sunlit silence. Hov'ring there,
I've chased the shouting wind along and flung
My eager craft through footless halls of air.
Up, up the long delirious, burning blue
I've topped the wind-swept heights with easy grace,
Where never lark, or even eagle flew;
And while with silent lifting mind I've trod
the high untrespassed sanctity of Space,
Put out my hand, and touched the face of God.

—John Gillespie Magee

If the sky beckons *you*, heed its call.

Answers to Ten Common Questions About Soaring

Question #1

Where can I obtain information about soaring in my area?

Answer

The Soaring Society of America maintains a list of clubs and commercial operations throughout the United States, available to anyone on request, for $3.00, plus S&H. Contact them as follows:

SSA Merchandise Department
P.O. Box E
Hobbs, New Mexico, 88241
Phone (505) 392-1177
Fax (505) 392-8154

Ask for the *1995-96 SSA Directory of U.S. Soaring Sites and Services;* item number 60 0002. It wouldn't hurt to identify yourself as a prospective newcomer to the activity. If you call, ask about a list of State Governors and their phone numbers. These people maintain each state's soaring records, and are generally familiar with all the detailed soaring activity which takes place within a given state; they will be able to provide more detailed information than can the SSA.

Question #2

How expensive is soaring?

Answer

It depends. If all you want is a ride, the cost can vary from free at some clubs to $50 to $100 for an introductory ride at a commercial operation, perhaps more. If you are interested in taking lessons, like any seriously pursued hobby — from maintaining a fishbowl to quilting — soaring costs can add up. Although flight training costs will vary with the individual, the location and the time a person can devote to lessons, to obtain a license from scratch can be expected to cost around $2,000. Less, if you already have a pilot's license and will be adding a glider rating. Figure on spending around $100 per hour for instructor, plane rental and tows through a commercial fixed-base operation (FBO). Often FBOs will have "packages", e.g. a beginner-through-solo package, a solo-to-license package, a package for pilots transitioning from power, etc.

Clubs offer lower cost alternatives to those who might be more certain of enduring interest, primarily because most clubs use all-volunteer labor. Typically, clubs will have a joining fee ranging from nominal through several hundred dollars, monthly dues and tow-and-glider charges. Some clubs refund part of the joining fee when you leave.

Some clubs also offer family memberships or other special categories, depending on their needs and circumstances.

Question #3

How expensive are the gliders themselves?

Answer

Since many composite sailplanes are manufactured over-seas, prices of *new* planes fluctuate with the exchange rate, often dramatically. Since pilots new to the sport typically purchase *used* ships, this answer applies to used sailplanes with a trailer. Prices can range from around $5,000 to greater than $40,000 for single-seaters, more for two-seat-ers, self-launching sailplanes and the best of the super-ships. Schweizer 1-26s tend to range in price from $6,000 to $10,000. Single-seat, 15-meter, composite ships range in cost from $14,000 to $40,000, depending on how com-petitive they are perceived to be in their racing class. For the past five years, an average price for a noncompetitive ship has been from $15,000 to $22,000. Note that differ-ences in piloting skills vastly exceed differences in these glid-ers' performances. A pilot of average skill flying the latest 15-meter ship would finish well toward the bottom of a national contest, while a top-notch pilot would finish near the top of a contest, regardless of which 15-meter ship he flew.

Question #4

Why so much?

Answer

The design of any licensed aircraft is highly technical, their manufacture labor-intensive. Except in World War II, airplanes have never benefited from mass-production economies, and probably never will. Gliders also, by their nature of striving for maximum efficiency, require extensive aerodynamic and specialized structural engineering. For example, very few powered planes utilize laminar flow or negative flaps. In structural aeronautical applications, gliders pioneered composites. All of this, plus liability costs, contribute to price. As mentioned in the main portion of the book, many friends reduce costs by joining in partnerships or syndicates. Plans and kits for gliders of all performance categories are available for people of average mechanical aptitude and above-average persistence. And despite the many FAA practices which tend to pour cold water on all sport aviation, thanks to the efforts of the Experimental Aircraft Association and the FAA, gliders (and powerplanes) built from plans or kits are easily licensable in the United States, provided common-sense rules are followed. The U.S. is unique among the countries of the world in this regard.

Question #5

How long can you stay up?

Answer

On an average spring or summer soaring day, thermal flights of several hours are not uncommon. Once a pilot understands the basics of thermalling flight, flights are often terminated by pilot choice rather than by the absence of lift. The author's longest thermal flight has been for nine hours and 20 minutes, and his average flight length in the single-seater he flies is over 3 hours. Of course, lift induced by wind — whether ridge lift or wave lift — will exist so long as the wind blows. Once a pilot knows how to soar, his concern shifts from how long he can stay up to how he can meet the needs of comfort and nutrition while he *is* up!

Question #6

What's it like, really quiet?

Answer

Next to the myth that wind is needed in order to go soaring, "quiet" is the next most popular myth. Compared to all powered flight, yes, soaring is quiet . . . very quiet. Compared to silence, soaring is surprisingly noisy because of the hiss of wind outside the cockpit. Trainers and two-seaters tend to be noisier than single-seaters because of the two-seaters' extra air leaks. Nonetheless, normal conversations are easily carried on in gliders at normal flying speeds. As for what it's like, the best single-sentence answer the author has encountered is, "It's like a whole 'nother world." One of the author's goals for this book has been to give the reader a fair idea of "what it's like."

Question #7

How difficult is it to learn how to fly?

Answer

Flying is like any other physical skill which can be learned by most reasonably coordinated humans. Unlike the Hollywood stereotype, pilots are not supermen; those who might think they are tend to kill themselves from a misjudgment or scare themselves into a more sensible perspective or hobby. At altitude, anyone can fly an airplane or a glider; the skill becomes necessary on takeoffs and, even more so, on landings, when the ground is nearby. Some experienced flight instructors (not all) will admit they have instructed people who just cannot seem to get the hang of flying, but these people seem to be the exception rather than the norm. A much larger percentage of flight instruc-

tors will agree that dangerous *attitudes* in students are much more common than lack of *aptitude*. There is nothing inherently dangerous about flight, but to a degree greatly exceeding driving or most other earthbound sporting activities, it demands respect, for it's terribly unforgiving of certain mistakes.

Question #8

How dangerous is soaring?

Answer

First of all, don't take just the author's word for it; your life is too valuable. Ask this question of everyone who participates in the sport. Also ask them how experienced they are so you get an idea of how informed or ignorant they may be.

In the author's opinion the most dangerous aspect of soaring is the drive to and from the airport, during which you are exposed to many more serious risks beyond your control than you are during flight. Presuming the absence of bad luck ("fate"), the risks which tend to kill pilots are risks they've deliberately chosen to take, such as flying into deteriorating weather or failing to fly coordinated in the pattern. If a person recognizes that any time they go faster than they're willing to hit a brick wall, or higher than they're willing to fall, they're taking life-threatening risks, soaring flight becomes a matter of managing the risks to keep them at an acceptable level. Risk management is a matter of education and flight instruction.

The gliders themselves are very rugged. They land at very slow speeds for airplanes, and there is no fuel to burn in the event of a crash. Unlike most powered flight, seat and shoulder belts are routinely used, as are parachutes in single-seaters since their seat pans are designed for them. The planes are inspected before each flight and an-

nually are inspected more extensively by an airplane mechanic (a requirement of the FAA).

Very few soaring accidents — regardless of severity — are a result of "fate." By far the largest percentage are a result of pilot error. The most dangerous aspect of soaring is the pilot. If you can control yourself, you can safely control a glider.

Question #9

How old does a person have to be to get a soaring license?

Answer

Instruction can begin as soon as the student can reach the flight controls in the glider and the instructor believes the student mentally mature enough to warrant the effort. The FAA permits solo flight any time after a student's 14th birthday, whenever the instructor believes the student ready (an indirect indication of how safe the government considers soaring). At age 16, a person can obtain a license, after which they can carry nonpaying passengers. People in their 80s have obtained licenses, and others of the same age have continued to instruct.

Question #10

What about a medical?

Answer

No medical examination is required in order to obtain a soaring license. Before a license will be issued, the applicant will have to sign a statement to the effect they have no physical or mental limitations which will prevent the safe operation of a glider. Once a license is obtained, flight

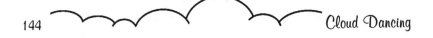
privileges are allowed so long as the statement continues to hold true. While a person *could* lie about this, the person they put most at risk is themselves. Similarly, in the event of an accident, should the insurance company get wind of a medical problem, your insurance might be void. Why do it? Besides, isn't it refreshing to be trusted by the government?

Common Soaring Terms

Introduction

*Although an attempt was made to avoid the use of glider pilots'
jargon throughout this book, by trying to define terms when and
where first used, there were a few exceptions (e.g. pitot and static
pressure). In any case, the reader might find helpful the following partial reference to some soaring words which were used
throughout the book and are likely to be heard at any soaring site.*

Achievement Badges — a term describing the internationally
recognized Silver, Gold and Diamond soaring badges administered by the Soaring Society of America (SSA) for the French-
based International Aviation Federation (FAI). (see FAI, SSA,
Silver Badge, Gold Badge, Diamond Badge)

Adverse Yaw — the condition existing when the nose of the
sailplane swings (yaws) the opposite direction (adversely) to that
intended by the pilot using aileron to begin a turn. Because of
their long wings, gliders tend to have lots of "adverse yaw." It's
caused by the aerodynamic drag of the ailerons being unequal;
the one displaced toward the ground creates more drag than the
one displaced toward the sky. The yaw string unhesitatingly re-
ports the presence of adverse yaw in sailplanes. The rudder is

used to counteract adverse yaw. (see Aileron, Drag, Rudder)

Aileron — the movable flap near the tip of each wing's trailing edge which, when moved, changes the amount of lift the tip of the wing produces, thereby controlling the glider's banking angle and rate of turn. The aileron is connected to the control stick in the cockpit. In automobile terms, ailerons are the glider's steering wheel. All airplanes have ailerons or something closely equivalent. (see Elevator, Rudder)

Barograph — a recording altimeter. No FAI soaring badge will be issued without corroborating proof in the form of a barograph; sometimes additional proof (e.g. photographs) is required. Most soaring clubs own several in order to encourage their members to attain higher levels of piloting skills. (see FAI, SSA, Silver Badge, Gold Badge, Diamonds)

Base — refers to a specific leg of a landing pattern, the next to last one, during which the sailplane's track is generally perpendicular to the runway on which it will soon land. "Base leg" is the last chance you get to shorten the pattern in the event you're low. Screw up a base leg and the short arrival (or crash) will happen much closer to the runway, but at least one big mistake will have been made much earlier. The newspapers will report something vaguely resembling the truth, usually pointing the finger of blame at the airplane or the weather. The pilot will know better (assuming he survives). (see Landing Pattern, Crosswind, Downwind, Final)

Blue Day — in soaring, any day without any clouds to mark locations of thermals. "Blue days" can be quite soarable; "blue holes" are another thing entirely.

Blue Hole — a term having meaning only on a convective soaring day. If the convection is strong enough to cause fair-weather cumulus clouds, a "blue hole" is an area marked by a distinct absence of clouds. Blue holes are treated with caution by soaring pilots because they often mark regions of little or no lift. Glider pilots flying cross-country hate to be "shot down by a blue hole."

Clearance — as used in this book, clearance is the minimum legal separation allowed between a sailplane and a cloud. This is one of the many things specified by the FAA in the FARs. (see FAA, FAR)

Cloud Soaring — the original term from the late 1920s given to what is today called thermal soaring. When thermals were first discovered, it was thought they existed only beneath clouds. As it became known updrafts could exist in the absence of clouds, the term "cloud soaring" evolved, until today it tends to mean flight within a cloud. In the U.S. today, thermal soaring is commonplace, soaring inside of clouds relatively uncommon; in Great Britain with its weaker, maritime-influenced lift and subsequently lower cloud bases, "cloud soaring" is much more common, almost a necessity.

Cloud Street — an alignment of fair-weather cumulus clouds into bands distinct from the more common random pattern. Cloud streets typically form on days when a steady wind is blowing and can be aligned parallel to or perpendicular to the wind. If they are aligned in the direction the soaring pilot wants to go, flight is simplified. Stronger cloud streets sometimes enable a sailplane to fly for miles without needing to stop and circle in a thermal to climb. Really strong ones can try and suck gliders into them; every glider pilot dreams of such cloud streets.

Composite (glider) — a catchall term applied to all sailplanes built using fiber-reinforced-plastic material. Fiberglass is the most common fiber, followed closely by carbon (graphite), then aramid (e.g. KEVLAR). Any all-white sailplane with sleek, swoopy lines is probably built at least partially of composites.

Crab Angle — the wonderfully descriptive term applied to the condition which exists whenever a glider's track across the ground differs from the direction its nose is pointed; caused by the effect of wind. It's normally noticed by the beginner only immediately prior to landing on a runway which is under the influence of a crosswind. It comes about because gliders (and airplanes) must angle into the wind slightly if they are not to drift to the downwind side of the runway under the effects of the breeze. Balloons always drift downwind; sailplanes fly with a crab angle any time they're not going directly upwind or downwind.

Crosswind — in this book, refers to one specific leg of the landing pattern, the first one, flown perpendicular to the runway on which the pilot intends to land. The term originates from the fact that the effect of low level wind in which the sailplane must land is generally coming from one side or the other of the glider, tending to drift it crosswise to the runway during this portion of the landing pattern. Additionally, pilots refer to any wind drift not directly along their flight track as a crosswind. A crosswind from directly ahead is called a headwind, from directly behind, a tailwind. Most pilots will swear they've never experienced a tailwind! (see Landing Pattern, Crosswind, Downwind, Base)

Cumulus Cloud — a type of cloud which forms as a result of rising air, cooling as it rises, causing the water vapor, which is always in the air, to condense into visible moisture. Fair-weather cumulus look like flat-bottomed cottonballs or popcorn. When upper air conditions are just right, small fair-weather cumulus will continue to grow vertically, creating towering cumulus, which will often presage a thunderstorm. (see Overdevelopment)

Dead Air — a soaring term meaning air that is neither rising nor falling. To the soaring pilot "dead air" is useful only for explicit and specialized performance testing of sailplanes or to grouse about on days when soaring is the goal.

Diamonds (aka Diamond Badge) — the highest of the three most common internationally-recognized soaring awards administered by the FAI. Strictly speaking, there is no such thing as a "Diamond Badge." Instead there are 3 diamonds to be worn around the perimeter of the "Gold Badge." Soaring pilots rarely bother with the distinction; you needn't either! As explained more fully in the text: Diamond Altitude requires a climb of 5,000 meters (16404 feet) after release from tow; Diamond Distance requires a flight of 500 kilometers (310.7 miles) after release; Diamond Goal requires a 300 kilometer (186.4 mile) flight to a pre-declared goal. As ship and pilot performances increase, it may eventually prove desirable to create additional badges; for now, you'll really have to work to gain your diamonds. (see FAI, SSA, Gold Badge, Silver Badge)

Downwind — refers to one specific leg of the landing pattern, usually the second one for gliders; can also refer to a "positional" state, as in "the glider was downwind of the ridge." Because sensible glider pilots always want to make their touchdown into any breeze which might be blowing at ground level, the "downwind leg" of the landing pattern gets its name from the fact that the breeze is tending to hasten your glider over the ground . . . if you've turned the correct way! Turning the wrong way onto "downwind" is often the first big mistake in the chain of mistakes leading up to an accident. (see Landing Pattern, Crosswind, Base, Final)

Drag (aerodynamic) — the resistance felt by all objects immersed in moving air, whether sailplane or car or building. Buildings resist drag by bulk. Cars tend to put up with it. Gliders attempt to minimize it. Kids like to play with it by sticking their hands out of car windows. Curiously, the simple creation of lift also creates drag. Thus when an aileron creates the additional lift required to roll a glider into a turn, it also creates additional drag thereby simultaneously creating adverse yaw. At the other wingtip, the decrease in lift of the oppositely-deflected aileron reduces the drag at that tip, further compounding the tendency to yaw adversely.

Elevator — the movable flap on the trailing edge of the smaller horizontal stabilizer surface at the tail end of the glider. The function of the elevator is to change the lifting force of the horizontal stabilizer and thereby change the pitch attitude of the glider, which changes the glider's speed. The elevator is connected to the control stick and is the glider's throttle. Some gliders move the entire horizontal stabilizing surface instead of just the trailing edge. (see Aileron, Rudder)

FAA — *F*ederal *A*viation *A*dministration. The federal bureaucracy evolved from its predecessor of the 1930s; its charter is to promote aviation and aviation safety throughout the United States. Most would agree it has performed the latter with more zeal than the former. Some would say to the detriment of the former. The FAA is God.

FAA Examiner — God personified to a would-be soaring pilot. An FAA Examiner (or an FAA Designee, a suitably qualified private individual to whom the FAA has granted the power) is the person you must convince you can safely and competently operate a sailplane prior to being issued a glider rating.

FAI (*F*ederation *A*viation *I*nternationale) — the French-based organization which certifies international aviation records, ranging from Charles Lindbergh's crossing of the Atlantic, to Dick Rutan and Jeana Yeager's non-stop globe encircling flight, to international soaring records. The FAI was formed in France a few years after the Wright brothers first opened the sky . . . once it was recognized aviation actually had a future. Why France? There, aviation was a Big Deal; in the U.S. the Wrights were still being scoffed at.

FAR — *F*ederal *A*viation *R*egulation. The codified form of the FAA's regulation of airplanes and airmen. All licensed pilots are responsible for being knowledgeable of the portions of the FARs which apply to the type of flying they do, including glider pilots. Written and oral tests must be passed before any license is issued. The FARs are the Ten Commandments on hormones.

Final — in flying, the last leg of an airplane's landing pattern. When done properly, the end result of a "final" is an uneventful landing. When things go wrong or the pilot screws up, the end result of a "final" is luridly described in the media. (see Landing Pattern, Crosswind, Downwind, Base)

Finish Gate — a line gliders flying contest tasks must cross in order to be considered to have completed the task. If a glider lands without flying or rolling through the finish gate — which can be anywhere on the airfield the contest organizers deemed necessary in the interest of safety — its score is penalized.

Flaps — In a general sense, flaps are any moveable portion attached to the trailing edge of an airfoil, whether main wing, horizontal stabilizer or vertical stabilizer. In a specific sense the term usually applies to that portion of the main wing trailing edge inboard of the ailerons. In gliders, unlike in most power-planes, flaps often move both up and down, benefiting performance at high speeds and low speeds respectively. Gliders use flaps at all speeds, from landing to thermalling to high speed running. The first time you see a glider landing exclusively with the aid of large deflection flaps (no spoilers), you'll think it's crashing, so steep is the approach. (see Aileron, Elevator, Rudder)

Flare, Landing — the transition from constant airspeed at decreasing altitude flight of the final approach to constant altitude at decreasing airspeed flight. When you "flare" a glider, you're bleeding off the extra safety airspeed carried throughout the landing pattern, in order to touch down at the slowest possible speed relative to the ground. Your tire will thank you every time for a properly performed flare, since it has to spin up instantaneously from zero rpm to whatever your touchdown speed is; so will your back.

Flight Examiner — this person is God personified to the would-be pilot. The flight examiner can be either an FAA employee, or a person designated by the FAA. This is the person who evaluates the aspiring pilot's knowledge of the FARs and flying skills, prior to agreeing, as the FAA's representative, to grant the applicant a pilot's license. (see Rating)

Formation Flight — what the Navy's Blue Angels do at airshows. Strictly speaking any time two planes are flying sufficiently close that one pilot feels compelled to continuously monitor the location of the other, formation flight is occurring. In gliding, every launch is a formation flight of two; thermalling in the company of other sailplanes is another form of formation flight.

Gold Badge — the middle of the three most common internationally-recognized soaring awards administered by the FAI. As explained more fully in the text: Gold Duration requires a 5-hour soaring flight; Gold Altitude requires a climb of 3,000 meters (9843 feet) after release from tow; Gold Distance requires a flight of 300 kilometers (186.4 miles). (see FAI, SSA, Diamonds, Silver Badge)

Groundloop — a term describing an inadvertent rotation about a plane's vertical axis during takeoff or landing. Pilots hate them. A groundloop can range from harmless to highly expensive and life-threatening. In gliders, groundloops on takeoff are usually the result of a bad wing run and are not very common. Landing groundloops in gliders are more common, due to their long wings, typically occurring on an off-field landing when the wingtip contacts the ground or tall grass before the plane can be braked to a halt. The prudent glider pilot works very hard to avoid groundloops. Due to their low takeoff and landing speeds, glider groundloops are rarely life-threatening, although fuselages are

another matter. Generally, only lower-speed airplanes groundloop; in higher-speed planes, they're called crashes. (see Wingrun)

Inversion (temperature) — a term used to describe a condition of the atmosphere when the air temperature rises with increasing elevation above ground. A temperature inversion will put a cap on thermal convection when the upper air temperature is warmer than the temperature of the rising air in the thermal. Often, you can see the effects of a temperature inversion by watching smoke early in the morning; if there is an inversion, the smoke will rise to the inversion, then spread horizontally.

Laminar Flow — a type of airflow in which little to no mixing takes place between molecules. Glider designers strive mightily to endow their creations with large areas of laminar flow. Being less turbulent than normal airflow, it's less draggy, hence its appeal.

Landing Pattern — the descending rectangular path followed by sailplanes (and powerplanes and commercial airliners) when returning to earth. Generally, the more consistent the landing pattern's path and airspeed, the more likely a smooth touchdown will occur. Even birds fly an abbreviated landing pattern; they generally make an abbreviated circle into the wind just before touchdown. Those that choose to land with a tailwind component tend to make really ugly landings, especially the larger ones. For cheap entertainment, watch birds landing in a wind! (see Crosswind, Downwind, Base, Final)

Lenticular Cloud — a high altitude cloud which forms in the presence of atmospheric waves; in cross section they're lens shaped. Small ones may have been mistaken for UFOs. Glider pilots often call lenticular clouds "lennies;" lennies aloft mean "surf's up!" to a glider pilot. To the average power pilot, lennies are either completely overlooked or feared. To the non-flying public, lenticular stacks make for spectacular sunrises and sunsets.

Lift — what glider and airplane wings create. To a glider pilot though, "lift" is the general term applied to air rising faster than the sailplane is sinking. It takes surprisingly little "lift" to keep a glider aloft. Most gliders sink about 200 feet every minute they circle in thermals. If you pace off 200 feet on the ground and walk at a pace to cover the distance in one minute, on a still day, you'll barely feel the breeze on your cheek.

Lift, Ridge — rising air created by wind flowing up and over hills, ridges and mountains. In the early days of soaring, the longest flights were mostly made in ridge lift; soaring history repeated itself in the two decades beginning in the late 1960s when the Allegheny ridges were "discovered." Today once again, for record purposes, the ridges may be in the process of being "outdistanced."

Lift, Rotor — lurking beneath the ethereal laminar smoothness of wave lift is "the rotor," a turbulent seething churning horizontal maelstrom. It's the atmospheric equivalent of what a surfer feels when unfortunate enough to fall off his board and sink beneath the surface of his wave. Treated with the utmost respect by sailplane pilots, the "up half" of rotors can often be used to climb into the wave itself. Rotors have been known to destroy gliders, lightplanes, and commercial airliners; they are suspected in the loss of military fighters. They are not for the beginner.

Lift, Shear — rising air created by a heavier air mass sliding beneath a lighter one, or a lighter one riding over a more dense one. In the U.S. shear lift is routinely used by glider pilots flying in the Mojave Desert; in the afternoons marine air flows from the LA basin into the Mojave via several mountain passes, often creating distinct lines of "shear cumulus." In other portions of the country, long soaring flights have been made in the shear lift ahead of fast-moving cold fronts and, occasionally, that of thunderstorm squall lines.

Lift, Thermal — the most common form of lift used by gliders. Thermals are the result of convection caused by sunlight's uneven heating of the ground in turn heating air above the hot spots, the warm air rising much like heated steam from a teakettle. Fair-weather cumulus mark the location of active or former thermals; thunderstorms are more dramatic evidence of strong thermals. (see Cumulus Cloud)

Lift, Wave — a form of lift caused by air flowing continuously over an obstruction, usually a mountain or large hill. Waves form in the atmosphere *downwind* of the obstruction, much like the ripple which forms behind a rock in a stream. Waves are known to extend to 100,000 feet, which is much higher than humans can survive without pressure suits.

Longeron — in an airplane or glider, a load-carrying, structural, longitudinal member in the fuselage. Only steel-tube and fabric, some wooden and some aluminum gliders have longerons. Composite sailplanes and sailplanes whose exterior skins carry flight loads lack longerons. Longerons in a glider are like a frame in a car. Similar to composite sailplane designs which lack longerons, many cars today lack frames, their loads being carried by the sheet metal itself.

Maneuvering Speed — in an airplane or glider, it is the speed below which any rapid and complete movement of the flight controls to their limits will not result in structural damage. If the engineers calculated their structural analyses correctly, below maneuvering speed the only way to kill yourself in a glider is to hit the ground. Above maneuvering speed, you can bend things permanently and, if going fast enough, pull the wings off. This is true of all airplanes, with the possible exception of military fighters, in which you'll black out before you damage the airframe.

Max L/D — (pronounced "max ell over dee") is the shallowest glide ratio of which any sailplane is capable; in still air, it occurs at one specific, unvarying, speed. The indicated airspeed of max L/D will vary depending on the vertical speed of the air through which the glider is flying. Dealing with this sort of esoterica is one of the charms, attractions, and — sometimes! — frustrations of being a sailplane pilot. Typical 2-seat training gliders in the U.S. have a max L/D in the low to mid 20s. Sailplanes having max L/Ds in the upper 30s are considered high performance by most sport sailplane pilots.

Microburst — an extremely localized occurrence of descending air, usually the result of a violent downdraft associated with a thunderstorm. Upon contact with the ground, microbursts (aka downbursts) spread out horizontally to cause strong horizontal wind shears, which have caused jetliners to crash. Once their existence was proven in the late 1970s and early 1980s, training and operating procedures were changed to minimize their hazards to commercial traffic. The rest of us must rely upon skill and luck to avoid them.

Min Sink — generally refers not to the actual minimum rate of vertical descent of the sailplane, but to the horizontal speed at which this is achieved. Min sink occurs at a slightly slower speed than max L/D, and is the speed at which you seek to fly the sailplane when in lift in order to maximize your rate of climb. Effectively, the speed of min sink is the slowest speed above stall speed at which the glider can be consistently controlled. Flying at min sink often gives transitioning power pilots the heebie jeebies.

Netto — a German word meaning "net." We wouldn't use it if it were not for the fact so many glider advances are from Germany. A netto variometer display shows what the air around the sailplane is doing. Surprisingly, even though this is precisely what every soaring pilot really wants to know, until Wil Schuemann put theory into practice, variometers showed what the *glider* was doing *relative to the air*. That's useful when you're climbing, but less so at higher speeds; a netto is immediately useful at *all* speeds. Even so, old habits die hard, and netto variometer displays are less common than they should be.

Oilcan — the term given to the sound made by aluminum glider wings flexing in turbulence. Schweizer gliders in particular oilcan quite a bit. Alarming at first, oil canning is perfectly harmless structurally, and soon becomes kind of a soothing background song the glider sings to the pilot. With experience, you can actually use the sound as an indication of a nearby thermal!

Oral (Test) — half of the test given prospective glider pilots by the FAA Examiner or FAA Designee; it generally hammers on the points of the written in which the candidate showed the least understanding. Few candidates are flunked on the oral, though many manage to fail the written test first time around, and some fail in airmanship during the final — flying — portion of the test.

Overdevelopment — a condition when fair-weather cumulus grow in size and coalesce. Serious overdevelopment is known as a thunderstorm.

Pilot-in-Command (PIC) — PIC is the guy at whom the Feds (and the lawyers) point the finger in the event of an incident or (shudder) an accident. Viewed from *your* perspective, assuming the mantle of pilot-in-command will forever change your concept of being "driver-in-command" of an automobile. It is a responsibility not to be taken lightly.

PIO — *P*ilot *I*nduced *O*scillation. In gliders, an up and down flight path aided and abetted by the pilot in his attempts to keep the flight path level. PIOs typically occur on a pilot's initial flight in a new type of sailplane at takeoff. Following the initial aft movement of the stick to lift the plane from the runway, if the plane rises higher than the pilot intends, a (typically unnecessary) corrective forward motion on the stick is made. Often the forward motion is even more excessive, and, alarmed by the low-altitude dive for the ground, the pilot pulls back stick much more enthusiastically than at liftoff. He is now out of phase, in a PIO. Trying to stop a PIO by "chasing the plane's motion with the stick" is very bad news indeed. Serious crashes have resulted, potentially fatal to glider pilot and tow pilot. Mild PIOs, consisting of two or three oscillations, are common on a pilot's initial flight in a new type of glider when the pilot is establishing the hand-eye feedback loop between stick motion and resultant glider motion. Serious PIOs are usually the result of insufficient or forgotten training. The driving equivalent to a PIO is overcorrecting a skid on an icy surface.

Preflighting — is the inspection performed by every prudent pilot before entering any airplane with intentions of being pilot in command (PIC). It's the flying equivalent of giving your car its annual inspection before you load it up for a long driving vacation. Proper preflighting technique is taught during flight training, but there's no substitute for a healthily skeptical eye. In gliders, it's highly unusual to find something seriously amiss, but the first time you do will make you a True Believer! In broad outline, preflighting is nothing more than a general look to verify that all the proper parts are there, will remain there, and are functioning properly; it's also a look to see that *improper* parts are *not* there. Critters are notorious for using sailplanes as homes . . . and morgues! (see Pilot-in-Command)

Pressure, Dynamic — is really a pressure *difference* between total pressure and static pressure. When objects have motion relative to the air (or any other fluid), they feel an immersion pressure from the fluid itself (static pressure) and a pressure from their motion through the fluid (total pressure). The pressure difference is a function of the object's speed relative to the fluid. In gliders, dynamic pressure is proportional to airspeed.

Pressure, Static — is the pressure exerted by the atmosphere on all objects at rest within it. Because air has weight, static pressure is higher at sea level than in Colorado, or any other point higher than sea level. The only time most non-pilots pay any attention to static pressure is when their ears pop.

Pressure, Pitot — is the pressure exerted by the atmosphere on an object in motion, at the exact spot where some poor air molecule is so crushed by his fellows that he cannot move in any direction . . . sort of the air's equivalent to the people at the riot at a rock concert who can't escape out the sides of the mob. The pressure caused by the motion of the object can be no higher than at this spot. Henri Pitot (pea' toe) was a French physicist (1695-1771) who invented a tube which simultaneously stopped fluids in motion (at the front of the tube, causing the riot) while also allowing it to flow smoothly past openings in the side of the tube (where static pressure was sensed). Called a *pitot tube* when used on airplanes, it allows measurement of the plane's speed through the air. (see Dynamic Pressure)

Pressure, Total — another term for pitot pressure. Total pressure is more descriptive of what's happening.

Rating — the FAA's term for their approval to fly different sorts of airplanes. When a pilot passes his very first flight test, he is issued a Pilot's License with the "Rating" for that particular test. For the persnickety or jargoons, no one really has a glider pilot's license, they have a pilot's license with a glider rating. Those who learn to fly in powerplanes first have a pilot's license with a single-engine-land rating. Other ratings include: multi-engine, instrument, seaplane, commercial, instructor, helicopter, etc.

Redline — a term descriptive of the maximum allowable speed of a glider or airplane, so called because it is marked on the airspeed indicator with a red line. The fastest way to become a test pilot is to fly faster than redline.

Release Altitude — the exact point at which the glider departs formation flight from behind the tug and enters its true element. The choice of release altitude is the pilot-in-command's, except in the rare event of an emergency. Generally, if not involved in a training flight, the PIC releases as soon as he or she determines they can stay up given the conditions of the moment. A typical release altitude on a thermal day might range from 2,000 to 3,000 feet above airport elevation.

Rudder — is the movable flap at the very rear of the glider, connected to pedals at the very front, and operated by the pilot's feet. Unlike the rudder in a boat, the rudder in a glider *does NOT* turn the glider, but is used primarily to keep the fuselage aligned into the airflow past the fuselage whenever the ailerons are used to bank the airplane. Without a rudder, gliders would happily try to fly sideways when banked into or out of turns by the ailerons. The rudder can also be used purposefully to make the glider fly sideways on a landing approach. There is no automobile equivalent of the rudder. Rudder control is probably the most difficult thing for newcomers to gliders to understand and use properly. (see Aileron, Elevator)

Sick Sack — like seat belts in a car . . . a good idea you hope you never *have* to use. Most multi-place gliders routinely carry a few because of the glider's marked response to atmospheric motion, and, the effect steep banks have on some folks unused to the sensations of soaring flight. 'T'is better to have used a sick sack and tossed, than never to have tossed at all . . .

Silver Badge — one of the three most common internationally-recognized soaring awards administered by the FAI; typically the first badge you will pursue. As explained more fully in the text: Silver Duration requires a 5-hour soaring flight; Silver Altitude requires a climb of 1,000 meters (3281 feet) after release from tow; Silver Distance requires a flight of 50 kilometers (31.1 miles). Once you've accomplished these goals, they may not seem too difficult, but from the other side of the skill fence, they're genuinely daunting! (see SSA)

Slip — in soaring, an intentional miscoordination between rudder and aileron, usually performed on final approach to landing as a means of getting rid of unneeded altitude. When rudder opposite to aileron is used (e.g. left aileron and right rudder), the nose of the glider will swing sideways to its flight path through the air, adding the drag of the fuselage to the overall drag of the normally coordinated airframe. To the uninitiated, slips look like incipient crashes.

Spoilers — are movable portions of the wing which can be operated by the pilot to project out from the wing into the airstream. Spoilers come in widely varying shapes and may be used on the top or bottom or both surfaces of the wings. The purpose of all of them is to destroy some of the wings' lift and create drag; they are used most commonly on landing approaches but might be used under a particularly strong cloud street to keep the glider from climbing into the clouds. Without spoilers, modern gliders would require huge airports because of their flat gliding angle at landing-pattern speeds.

SSA (*S*oaring *S*ociety of *A*merica) — a nonprofit national organization of soaring enthusiasts which seeks to foster and promote all phases of gliding and soaring on a national and international basis. Most soaring nuts' contact with the SSA comes via its monthly magazine and the service it provides in validating soaring badge applications with the International Aviation Federation (FAI). Founded in 1932, SSA additionally sanctions regional and national soaring contests, encourages uniform standards for soaring instruction, serves as a clearinghouse for soaring information and knowledge, has sponsored sailplane design contests, serves as the unified voice of soaring enthusiasts whenever it's necessary to joust with the Feds, and more. Not every soaring pilot or club member is an SSA member — but they should be — simply because of the magazine which will help make them a better, safer pilot.

Stall — in gliding, the term refers to the condition reached when the wing can no longer sustain the weight of the sailplane. This happens when the wing is angled too steeply into the oncoming air flow. Though thought of by many sailplane pilots as a low speed phenomenon, stalls can occur at any airspeed and any attitude; all the wing knows is angle, not speed. Practicing stalls is a normal part of training. If left to its own devices, the sail-

plane would prefer to unstall itself in any case. The reason stalling has assumed such a prominent place in pilots' pantheon of war stories, is the consequences can be deadly if an unexpected stall occurs without sufficient altitude to effect a recovery. In gliders, several hundred feet is a lot of altitude to lose in the event of an inadvertent stall. Throughout much of the landing pattern, you don't have several hundred feet to waste; an inadvertent stall is then usually called a crash.

Start Gate — an invisible line in the sky employed at glider contests below which all gliders much pass before they are considered to be on course without being subject to a time penalty. The gate is established by simple geometric hardware on and monitored from the ground. Start gates are used to attempt to minimize the luck involved with takeoff time at contests. For something not directly related to soaring flight, start gates probably are the source of more controversy than anything else. The best way to learn about them is to ask every question which comes to mind in the event you get to witness a glider contest!

Sun Dog (Glory, Halo) — a circular rainbow which forms downsun of high-flying sailplanes against a cloud backdrop. Though not rare in the physics sense, few sailplane pilots ever get to see a sun dog, simply because in the U.S. it's uncommon for sailplanes to attain such a position. Those who see them, have gained a lasting memory.

Tip Vortices (Vortexes) — usually invisible swirls of air formed by all wings in the process of creating lift. Air leaking from the higher pressure bottom surface of the wing to the lower pressure upper surface streams behind the airplane in a form of manmade horizontal tornado. Tip vortices behind heavy jet airliners can be dangerous to aircraft following behind. In gliders, tip vortices are merely another form of drag; one reason gliders have long wings is to minimize the strength of tip vortices, because every smidgen of drag reduction is critical. How low is the drag of a glider? During an aerotow, you could easily hold the towrope in one hand if the glider pilot maintained proper position!

Transition Zone — in soaring, the mixing area between rising air of thermals and the air surrounding them. Often the glider pilot's first hint lift is nearby is a slight trembling of the air-

frame as the plane flies into this "nervous" air; actual lift doesn't show on the variometer until a few seconds after the plane itself begins rising. (see Oilcan)

Variometer — along with the yaw string, the most important instrument for soaring flight. Variometers are simply very sensitive rate-of-climb instruments. Human ears contain a very crude variometer, but not nearly good enough for soaring flight.

Visual Contact (with the ground) — something the loss of which is very bad news to the sport sailplane pilot (or any other non instrument-rated pilot)! Your sense of equilibrium exists only because you can see a distant horizon. For a graphic demonstration of what will happen to the unlucky/unwary pilot who loses "visual contact," have a friend help you perform the following demonstration. Seat yourself, blindfolded, in a revolving chair while your friend slowly and gently spins the chair in any manner of their choosing, while you verbalize to your friend which direction the chair is being rotated. It's a lot of fun, in a chair; a great party pastime. In an airplane, it's a matter of life and death.

Wave Window — a column of airspace beginning at 18,000 feet and extending up as high as controllers in the controlling En-Route Air Traffic Control Center permit. Wave windows are the means by which the FAA grants gliders access to airspace above 18,000 feet, the point at which gliders and controllers would otherwise have to comply with the more restrictive Instrument Flight Rule (IFR) regulations. Even when equipped with the electronic aids required by IFR regulations, gliders do not easily fit within the other restrictions of IFR flight, adding a burden onto "Center." Wave windows are an easily implemented compromise; other IFR traffic is simply routed to either side of the wave window column by "Center."

Weak Link — a smaller diameter, weaker length of rope containing a metal ring which attaches between the main towrope and the glider's tow release. Because overstrength towropes are normally used (to avoid frequent replacements made necessary due to abrasion when the rope drags across the ground on take-off and landing), weak links are inserted. This replaceable safety device is designed to ensure the connection between glider and towplane will break before structural damage occurs to either,

should the glider get so badly out of position large forces are induced in the towrope. The breaking strength of the weak link is one of the items specified in the FARs.

Wingrun — is what the person who connects the towrope to the glider does to assist the glider's takeoff. Because gliders have only a single wheel below the fuselage, at rest, they tilt onto one or the other wingtip, much as a bicycle rests on its kickstand. Because the ailerons do not function until air flows over them, the wingrunner levels the wings at the start of the takeoff roll. As the towplane accelerates the glider, the wingrunner allows the wingtip to rest on a palm until the glider is going faster than he can run, by which time the ailerons work normally.

Written (Test) — the first bureaucratic hurdle any prospective pilot must negotiate on the way to a private pilot's license. The glider written is actually quite straightforward, a thing easily passed by most. For example, if this book is your introduction to soaring, you could probably take the glider "written" and come close to passing without further study. Hmmm...

Yaw String — a piece of yarn or string taped to the centerline of the outside of the canopy. The yaw string is the least expensive, most sensitive and most reliable instrument gliders use. With the exception of an intentional slip, the glider pilot can fly no more efficiently than to keep the yaw string always pointed directly back at the rudder. Any plane without a propeller up front can benefit from a yaw string; two jets which use them are the U-2 and the supersonic F-14.

Zero Sink — a condition of the atmosphere in which the sailplane is neither rising nor falling; the air's upward motion exactly matches the glider's sink rate. Cloud streets can result in extended zero sink at high flight speeds. Other than allowing the glider to fly straight ahead without losing altitude, there's nothing special about zero sink, rather, the term is merely a convenient point of reference when describing flight conditions.

Basic Glider Structure

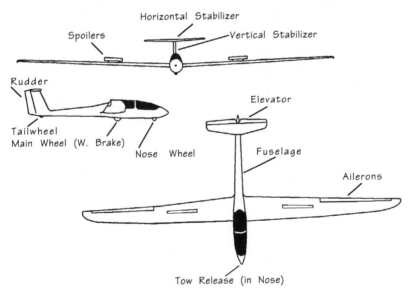

Horizontal Stabilizer

Spoilers

Vertical Stabilizer

Rudder

Elevator

Tailwheel
Main Wheel (W. Brake)

Nose Wheel

Fuselage

Ailerons

Tow Release (in Nose)

Grob G-103 Twin III Sailplane

Specifications

Wingspan	59 Feet
Empty Weight	928 Lbs.
L/D	36:1
Construction	Fiberglass/Resin Matrix
Manufacturer	Grob Werke GmbH & Co.

Suggested Reading

Interested in reading more? Below is an introduction to additional material. All are books with the exception of the first listing, a monthly magazine. Opinions expressed about each title are my own. Not all are currently in print, though most, if not all, are available in libraries. If your library doesn't have a particular title, ask if it can be had through inter-library loan. Additionally, current soaring-specific outlets for books in print can be obtained from the SSA. Also, almost any bookstore will be happy to special order these books for you, should you wish to include them in your soaring library. Enjoy!

Soaring — The Journal of the Soaring Society of America, Inc., This is a 60-page monthly magazine available through SSA. Printed on glossy stock in 8.5 x 11 format, it is internationally known in the soaring community. In addition to cover photos suitable for framing, each issue generally contains four or five feature articles on topics ranging in interest from the beginner to the advanced soaring pilot. I know of no better means of getting a feel for general soaring activity throughout the U.S. at any point in time than reading *Soaring*. Don't forget to check your local library; they may either subscribe to the magazine directly or be the recipient of a gift subscription from a soaring fan.

***America's Soaring Book, by The Editors of* Flying Magazine**, © 1974, 1975 by Ziff-Davis Publishing Co. Don't be put off by this book's hefty size. It merely reflects the wonderful breadth to be found in soaring; of course pictures — and a lot of them — are part of the package. At the not inconsiderable risk of committing criticism by brevity, this is an excellent, comprehensive, accurate, and *interesting* review of the American soaring scene. In it you'll find some history, along with insights into European soaring, basic training, contest flying, etc. Highly recommended as your next read beyond *Cloud Dancing*.

Go Fly a Sailplane — An Introduction to Soaring, © 1981 by Linda Morrow and Ray Morrow, Atheneum. Here is a wonderful book targeted at teens and youngsters with an interest in the sport, but adults will enjoy it too. It's a mix of the practical and the inspirational-by-example, yet it completely avoids unnecessary hype. The chapter on U.S. teenagers with demonstrated soaring skills and future aspirations is good stuff. The Morrows are a soaring family. The joy they found upon taking up the activity, and the respect they have as parents for good societal values they encountered in it, shows in this book. Well illustrated with photos.

Half Mile Up Without An Engine — The Essentials, the Excitement of Sailplanes & Soaring, by Robert Gannon, © 1982 by Prentice-Hall Inc. Probably available only through libraries. This is another excellent all 'round, introduction to the sport, covering some history, personal vignettes, training aspects, visits into the cockpits of sailplanes during record-breaking flights, etc. Many photographs.

Modern Soaring Guide, by Peter M. Bowers, © 1979 by TAB Books. Proving good things can come in small packages, this is an informative, well illustrated, detailed book about all aspects of the sport, written by an airplane designer, builder, pilot, sailplane pilot, and historian. Regrettably, a few of its many photos contain misidentified sailplane types . . . but can you find 'em?

With Wings as Eagles — The story of soaring, © 1975 by D. S. Halacy, Jr., Bobbs-Merrill Company, Inc. This is another informative, well-illustrated, easy-to-read natural follow-on to *Cloud Dancing*. Halacy is both an experienced writer and sailplane pilot, showing both to good effect herein.

Once Upon a Thermal, © 1974 by Richard A. Wolters, Crown Publishers Inc. Comes in and out of print; check your library. This book is roughly comparable in size to *Cloud Dancing*. Quoting from the dust jacket, its topic? "Soaring — the marvelously fun-filled and dramatic story of a man who took up gliding at forty-eight and lived to become a champion . . . of sorts." A wonderful and charming — yet accurate — introduction to the sport through the eyes of a raw beginner, who progressed in a few short years from flagpole sitting, to cross-country, to regional, and ultimately to national competition. At the time he took on the sport's challenge, Wolters was already a bestselling author. It shows in this book. His knack for communicating an amazing range of concepts clearly, simply, and — most important — entertainingly, will have you chuckling throughout the book.

The Art & Technique of Soaring, © 1971 by Richard A. Wolters, McGraw-Hill Book Company. If you encounter this book in a library, check it out. Though its target audience is the student pilot, it has many superb and intriguing photos anyone will enjoy.

Beginning Gliding, © 1975 by Derek Piggott, Barnes & Noble Import Division. This is a book directed at the beginning student. Written by a highly experienced sailplane pilot/instructor, it explains in the British style, the mechanics of controlling a sailplane. Keep it in mind if you decide to take up the sport. Illustrated by the author.

Understanding Gliding — The Principles of Soaring Flight, © 1977 by Derek Piggott, Barnes & Noble Import Division. Piggott's British style permeates this complement to the preceding book, lending it a comfortable, chatty air. In this book, Piggott goes beyond the basic mechanics of sailplane control and gives you the "whys" and "wherefores." Its earlier chapters will probably be of interest to most readers, while the later ones may be a bit too comprehensive for the casual reader. Still, it's worth a look! Many illustrations by the author.

Soaring With the Schweizers, © 1991 by William Schweizer, Rivilo Books. This book is a combination personal memoir and company history. Bill Schweizer is one of the three Schweizer brothers responsible for creating two generations of U.S. sailplanes. If you get hooked by the sport, you'll eventually want to add this book to your collection for its historical information alone. Photos and appendixes.

Wings Like Eagles — The Story of Soaring in the United States, © 1988 Smithsonian Institution, by Paul A. Schweizer, Smithsonian Institution Press. An awe-inspiring book in scope, for the beginner it's filled with historic photos and brief descriptions of historic soaring events, though it will definitely be a bit much to read in one sitting. It's an awesome reference book. Check it out of your library, though it's also readily available for purchase.

SOARAMERICA, © 1976 (and edited) by John Joss, The Soaring Press. This is a relatively unknown little gem, even among the *cognoscenti*, which is a shame because it's a

wonderful combination of travelogue and great flight stories by the participants. Where else will you find the story of an 18-year-old who soared a home-built sailplane 700 miles from southern Texas to northern Colorado? Each of the chapters originally appeared as an article in *Soaring* magazine. Possibly available via library or through the SSA.

Winning On the Wind, © 1974 by George B. Moffat, Jr., The Soaring Press. Available through SSA outlets. Quoting from the back cover, the book, ". . . is widely regarded as some of the finest writing ever on the magnificent sport of soaring. It has received acclaim from successful athletes in many other sports. It is also praised by professionals whose goal is excellence, because its principles for success work effectively in the game of life itself." All true, but how do you summarize 3 novella-length books in one? It will be the rare reader who doesn't find at least one section compelling reading. National and World Championship-winning Moffat, a high school English teacher by profession, writes in descriptive colors. Highly recommended.

About the Author

Robert F. Whelan is a Washington, D.C. native, raised and educated in Maryland. His formal education ended with a degree in aerospace engineering from the University of Maryland. Most of his adult life has been spent as a manufacturing engineer/jack of all trades working in the computer peripherals industry, sleeping, or playing in the sky. An experienced sailplane pilot/owner, Whelan believes the sport too wonderful to be kept a secret. He has lived where the plains meet the mountains since 1976.

Cloud Dancing
Your Introduction to Gliding and Motorless Flight

by Robert F. Whelan

Additional copies of *Cloud Dancing* can be had by doing any one of the following:

❖ calling, toll free, 1-800-356-9315, Visa/MC/Amex accepted

❖ faxing, toll free, 1-800-242-0036, Visa/MC/Amex accepted

❖ sending $14.95, plus $3.00 shipping and handling, plus applicable sales tax to Rainbow Books, Inc., P. O. Box 430, Highland City, FL 33846-0430.

❖ asking your local bookseller to order ISBNumber 1-56825-025-8

This entire page, as well as the cover of *Cloud Dancing*, can be modified to reflect your large-quantity, special purchase. Contact the Publisher, Betty Wright, at the above address for more information.